To Lupita

I hope you
stay as much as I
enjoyed living it.

Bill Myers
Soren Blau

Janet Worjewkeng

M000028386

Forever Blue

By
William David Myers
As told to
Janet Warford-Perry

Printed by BookMasters, Inc., Mansfield, Ohio

Copyright 2000 by Bill Myers and Janet
Warford-Perry

All rights reserved. No part of this book may be
reproduced in any form or by any means without
the prior written permission of the author, ex-
cepting brief quotations used in connection with
reviews, written specifically for inclusion in a
magazine or newspaper article.

Printed in the United States of America

First edition

Jacket design and illustrations by Bill Myers and
Janet Warford-Perry

This book is dedicated to all the men and women who proudly wore blue.

Contents   Page

Introduction

Standing outside the academy in 1998. Thirteen years following my retirement this place brings back fond memories.

When I proudly took the oath, promising to protect and serve the people of Los Angeles, I never envisioned the events I would witness during my career, most of which maybe no man should ever see.

Growing up in Afton, a small town in northeastern Oklahoma, I dreamed of one day becoming a police officer. So much so, when I grew to be a man, I never considered pursuing any other career.

Enlisting in the Navy during the summer following my tenure at Afton High School, I set sail on a new adventure in California, far removed from my rural upbringing.

While stationed on the aircraft carrier USS Hornet, my homeport was Long Beach, California, just a short stint down the freeway from the City of Angels.

It was there I met the woman who would support my dream of becoming a police officer. Shortly after Lupe and I married in 1964, I began attending Long Beach City College, then went off to test for the position as a Los Angeles police officer. The exams were many and very difficult. The first being an aptitude test, then came the agility test, followed by oral interviews (which I found out years later I scored 100 on), then a rigorous physical examination.

It took about eight weeks for background

checks to clear. I remember all of my neighbors and people I'd worked with would come up to me or call and say, "What have you gotten yourself into? Did you know the Los Angeles police have been to our house asking about you and your habits?"

But at last the big day came and on Sunday, May 19, 1968, I entered the Los Angeles Police Academy. With my head shaved like boot camp and wearing my kakis starched stiff, not a wrinkle to be found, shoes spit shined, this is where I would spend the next five months, while receiving 832 hours of college accredited police training.

Now chasing my boyhood dream had begun.

And chase I did. With vigor and gusto along the crime infested streets in the Watts district of Los Angeles, first as a rookie on a patrol beat. Tagged early on with the name of "Okie," I spent all of my waking hours in pursuit of robbers, rapists, gang fighters and domestic abusers.

I quickly climbed the ladder of success, working my way through patrol, then into the vice squad where I began the task of undercover investigation of gambling and prostitution rings, and as Lupe once said, "getting paid to drink and gamble all night with a bunch of guys."

In the early1970s, I entered an exciting new field, becoming a member of the newly formed Special Weapons and Tactics (SWAT) team, the first such group formed in America. During that time period there was much unrest in our country.

With the Vietnam War protest in full swing, college students were rioting, the civil rights movement was beginning, the war against communism raged and there was much talk about urban guerilla warfare. In addition, the Black Panthers were trying to "off-a-pig" and the spawning of the now famous gangs had originated in south central Los Angeles.

Yes most times, it was literally a war in the streets.

Today, Lupe and I enjoy a life with much less stress, but I haven't completely given up chasing childhood dreams. Retiring from the LAPD in 1985, because of a severe injury to my ankle and lower back, I continue to protect and serve, working as a lake patrolman for the Grand River Dam Authority on Grand Lake O' the Cherokees in northeastern Oklahoma.

And there is no hesitation whether or not I would do it all over again.

I've always told everyone, I loved my job

so much I would have worked as a police officer for free.

This is my story.

Chapter One

A boyhood dream

Ottawa County Sheriff's Force
Miami, Oklahoma

HORACE RIDER
Undersheriff

W. E. HUNNICUTT
Deputy

BEN STANLEY
Sheriff

CURTIS MYERS
Deputy

ARTHUR PECK
Deputy

My father Curtis Myers (pictured top row, fourth from right) spurred on a childhood dream of becoming a policeman.

I was born at home on August 18, 1942, to Esther and Curtis Myers, the eldest of three children.

My father ran a filling station on the old Route 66 highway in Afton. But it was his later occupation as a deputy under Ottawa County Sheriff Ben Stanley, which intrigued me.

My father later became a county commissioner for the next 30 years.

I believe my father's job in law enforcement, spurred on my dream. My dad, Curtis Myers worked county roads during the bootlegging heyday, and to me, my father's pursuit of revenuers, complete with high-speed chases, was very alluring. All of his stories were so exciting when he returned home from the end of a shift.

At the time my father was a deputy sheriff, Oklahoma was a "dry" state and Ottawa County was no exception. Situated in the northeast corner of the state, bootleggers had to travel through Ottawa County to get to bigger cities like Tulsa and Oklahoma City. Local law enforcement officers were always ready and anxious to pursue.

Roadblocks were set up late in the night to nab the bootleggers who came in caravans, with a front-runner, followed by a carrier of the whiskey in another car, with a tail car trailing behind. When the bootleggers met up with the law, sparks flew from the racing cars, inevitably the back driver would turn the car sideways and toss his keys into a nearby ditch and flee in an attempt to bring the pursuit to a halt.

Lots of cars were wrecked and many bottles of whiskey were broken in Ottawa County, I recall my father saying. Lawmen used their personal vehicles to chase the revenuers, but those days were so exciting, I always dreamed of becoming the cop who chased the bad guys.

When my father was off in the Navy during the war, my mother used to take me to see the picture shows. It seemed like everybody always loved the beat cop. He was always the good guy.

I always knew there had to be more to life than the streets of Afton, Oklahoma. At age 17, I begged my mother to let me join the Navy. She always refused the repeated requests, saying she would never sign the papers.

Ten days after my 18th birthday, in the summer of 1960, as an adult, I was free to join the Navy without any signatures. I just had to roam and see what that big world out there had to offer. I wanted to see what was on the other side of the wheat fields.

A tiny glimpse of worldly ways had been offered from Main Street in Afton, more commonly known today as Route 66. In those days, Afton was a prosperous town of 3,000 people compared to the population today that has dwindled to less than 1,000. Travelers from the railroad kept the growing town alive and Highway 66 always bore heavy traffic with vacationers and business people traveling from one coast to another. The small farming community grew, and in its heyday, the town proper boasted seven hotels, ten motels, four restaurants and a rotating railroad roundhouse that turned the steam engines around. There were two drugstores, a hospital, two grocery stores and several full service filling stations.

Working through the summer as a pressman, commonly known as a devil's helper, for the Afton American newspaper, I was convinced even more that I wasn't destined to stay in Afton.

On August 29, 1960 I enlisted in the U.S. Navy. My eyes filled with wonder at the massive sight—the USS Hornet aircraft carrier docked at its homeport in Long Beach. The ship was home to 4,000 military personnel when the air squadron was aboard, with the ship housing a full thousand people more than my hometown boasted in its heyday.

It wasn't long before this green horn was fulfilling his dream, enjoying exotic ports of call, Hawaii, Japan, Hong Kong, the Philippines as well as many ports along the western coast of the United States such as San Diego, San Francisco, and Brimington, Washington in the Pungent Sound.

The ship soon ventured along the coast of Vietnam to pick up Marine troops who were ready for rest and relaxation. The marines would tell sailors stories of the horrors of war in this country called Vietnam, a place none of us had ever heard of at that time. Of course that was before the war efforts were made public.

I remember looking forward to liberty shortly after dropping anchor in Hong Kong harbor. That is, until the ship's captain's voice came over the intercom and made a stern announcement.

"Make way to set sail," came the stern order.

The sailors cursed, moaned and complained at the thought of exiting this wonderful

Shortly after my 18th birthday, I joined the Navy to see the world.

paradise in the Orient.

Until we heard the news November 22, 1963, that our beloved President John F. Kennedy, who had been aboard the USS Hornets earlier in the summer, had been assassinated. The announcement was a first touch of reality for me. For up until now I was fully involved in enjoying seeing the world and all its glory.

During the four years I spent in the Navy, the ship returned many times to its homeport in Long Beach, California. I never realized how significant this place would become in the years to follow. I just cherished the opportunity to see something beyond my native homeland.

Less than a year into my Naval career, I met a Hispanic woman who would become my life's mate. Lupe's cousin owned a beer bar in Long Beach, a place where my Naval buddies and I frequented when in port. Spotting the pretty Mexican woman, I asked her cousin to introduce us.

Leery of jumping into a relationship after experiencing a miserable first marriage, Lupe was skeptical and kept herself at bay for quite some time. Finally agreeing to meet me at the picture show one afternoon, then reconsidering and deciding not to show. But as hours lingered on she called the movie theater and asked if there was anyone outside that appeared to be waiting.

To which the ticket agent replied, "There's a young man that's been walking back and forth out on the sidewalk out front for hours."

So Lupe drove by the theater to find me standing there on the corner. Feeling sorry for this Okie, she pulled to the curb and said, "Get in."

We never saw the movie that day, as the cat and mouse game continued long after the picture show began. That's when we went to have our first cup of coffee and I received my initial Spanish lesson.

Looking back on that first conversation with Lupe, I wonder why this pretty young lady ever took a second look at me, much less staying to raise the children while I played "cops and robbers."

I never will forget that first conversation over coffee.

"My name is Lupe," the attractive Hispanic woman greeted.

Since the woman pronounced her name "Loopie," I assumed, incorrectly, a nickname was used.

"What is your real name," I inquired.

"It's Lupe," came the reply, this time with impatience in her voice.

"You don't understand," I explained. "My real name is William, but everyone calls me Bill."

"No, you dumb ass, you don't understand," came the frustrated reply. "My real name is Lupe and that's what everybody calls me."

This time I comprehended, loud and clear. In the days that followed, I also understood this woman was definitely strong enough to hold her own in the difficult role as a police officer's wife.

Far removed from my background, Lupe's siblings included two brothers and five sisters, and a large extended family of aunts, uncles and cousins. Every event was a time for celebration and her family gathered often to honor each child's birthday, baptism, weddings, anniversaries and any other occasion they could find to celebrate and throw a party. No one was better at turning a small gathering into a gala event where the best food and drink were always served. The women would slave for hours over the stove, much to their guests' delight.

Not only was I accepted into a new family, I was also oriented on Mexican food and custom long before most gringos found Taco Bell.

Accustomed to big gatherings, Lupe's mother always had a pot of beans on the stove, homemade tortillas and fresh salsa that she served to visitors. The family rarely used the living room, but gathered around a big kitchen table, ate tortillas, drank coffee and visited. In many ways I was lonesome for my family back home and welcomed the opportunity to interact with Lupe's large family.

Three years of courtship later, on May 13, 1964, in a packed Los Angeles courthouse, a judge married Lupe and I alongside about 10 other couples, during his honor's lunch break. On August 28 of the same year, with four years commission in the Navy ending, we set sail on a new life together.

I was also in search of a job to provide for a ready-made family, Lupe and my two stepsons, Eddie and Carlos. Employment was low and work difficult to find. Lupe had already made one stipulation—any job would suit her fine as long as it paid over $2 per hour, which is what she figured it would take to support the family. She told me I could have anything over the $2 per hour to keep for myself—a portion she has since reneged on several years ago.

My first job was a one-day stint at Allen Industries, a manufacturer of automobile carpeting, but it did fit the monetary criteria. At $2 per hour, with major holidays paying double-time, I signed on with the firm Labor Day of 1964. But within four hours, I was close to finding myself the senior man left at the plant. Working conditions were horrendous due to the unbearable heat in the metal building with no air conditioning and little ventilation. After what seemed like the longest four hours of my life, the lunch wagon rolled around. I made a vow to an older co-worker: This would be my last day at the factory. The gentleman commented if he weren't so old, it would be his last day as well.

Making good on my promise to walk, I soon found myself at Richfield Oil Company, which later became Atlantic Richfield, working in the Wilmington refinery. My tenure was much longer than at Allen's, staying about four years, attending Long Beach City College on the side.

During this period of time my daughter Kelly was born on Sept. 22, 1965. Being only the second girl born in the Myers family, she was a little special to everyone.

I soon learned the LAPD was seeking new recruits, giving entrance exams daily. After taking the written test, I passed an oral interview, physical agility then waited patiently eight weeks for an extensive background check.

It was during this time the neighbors would hail to me saying, "Hey Okie, the police were here today asking about you."

One of the happiest days of my life came May 19, 1968, on a Sunday, when I was officially sworn in to join the Los Angeles police academy.

With a freshly shaven head, I embarked on rigorous law enforcement training that made Navy boot camp look like a boy scout hike in comparison. I never ran so hard or jumped so high or studied so many late hours. Every day the class ran several miles through Elysian Park near Dodger Stadium. Training included learning to deal with suspects mentally as well as physically.

Officers drove back and forth each day to class, on the freeway at four o'clock in the morning and if all went well, we were home by seven that evening.

Academy uniforms (kakis) had to be kept spotless and wrinkle-free, starched so stiff the garments could stand-alone. I was thankful for the previous military training in that area. A black gentleman acquaintance of Lupe's owned a dry cleaning service not far from our home. Mr. LaRue made sure the uniforms were cleaned and pressed, no matter what the hour of drop-off. I can remember him bringing my uniforms to me as late as midnight. If the truth were known, I wouldn't have had a law enforcement career had it not been for the friendship of Mr. LaRue. I'm not really sure if I ever properly thanked him enough for his diligence.

The kakis would be transported to the academy on a hanger. One would never dare wear his uniform for fear of developing a crease or wrinkle. We would then dress at the academy, making sure not to sit down or bend a leg. Inspection would be a 6 a.m. sharp on the parade field. Everyone was standing tall in his place. Now out of a class of well over 100, someone was sure to get a gig, have some fault in his appearance. Suddenly we would hear, "Maybe you guys need a little wake-up run this morning." Then it would be double time, up Cardiac Hill and back down again. I know that damned hill went straight up for at least a half-mile.

By the time we arrived at our first class, the now heavily soiled uniform was ready for the laundry once again but the day had only just begun. Sometimes the heavy starch would chap the insides of our legs but nobody dared complain for fear of hearing those words so often heard, "Bring your hat and books."

We all wondered if we would make it to graduation day. Cardiac Hill would also be double-timed if someone's eyelids drooped during class. No time for sleeping here, class work was far too important. Something you missed might cost an officer to lose his life or that of a citizen or partner.

Penal code, vehicle code, powers of arrest, and warrants, each code was recited one law at a time. A test was administered every week—pass it or the cadet wasn't in class the following week. Never take graft, money or anything that wasn't yours, know how to handle every situation an officer encountered, it was all drilled in at the academy.

Everything an officer does has a reason. For example, to this day, I never accept a driver's license in a plastic holder because money could be stuck inside the holder. Honesty protects everyone and if an officer follows what the academy teaches, trouble won't follow him.

I remember as though it was yesterday when an instructor explained to us the thin blue line theory. The thin blue line being the police officers throughout the United States repre-sented the thin blue line between good and evil and right and wrong. We were all so proud to have the opportunity to wear blue and take our places among the thin blue line.

Cadets lived in fear and the teaching was done with stress factors imposed. Students were scared at the thought of leaving a good job, wife and kids to join the academy. Starting back at zero would be the only option. Life is full of different types of situations—it prepared officers for stress on the streets.

At the time I thought it cruel and unusual punishment, particularly when the class began to dwindle rapidly from 140 students to 85. I hated the instructors during most of the 832 hours of training, but realized later, they saved my life many times over. Every officer that has ever lost his life in the line of duty saved other officers lives when they realized the mistakes made.

Failure to comply with all the rules and regulations of the academy was cause for imme-diate dismissal. There was a reason for the rigor; if you don't duck on the streets, you're dead. One poor guy was dismissed just as the class was getting dressed for graduation, after last-minute locker checks revealed live ammunition inside. Live ammunition was never allowed inside the facility, only on the firing range for obvious reasons. But apparently sometime during the five months of training, this officer went back to the locker with two live rounds in his pocket, discarding them in his locker where they were long forgotten. During the locker inspection the rounds were discovered and this officer's career ended in a split second—just moments before it was scheduled to officially begin.

Not a day went by that a training officer didn't kick open the door, holler a specific man's name, ordering him to get his hat and books, and the rest of the class never saw the cadet again.

We would spend hours on the firing range learning how to use our weapons. Thousands of rounds of ammunition were fired. Usually the last class of the day was in P.T. gear on the track. After warming up, we would go over all the control holds and moves. Over and over again we performed these holds on each other. It had to be practiced to perfection for once confronting actual suspects there was only one opportunity to gain control of the situation. We also learned what it felt like to be fully controlled by these holds. The bar-arm control, a choke-out hold, was probably used most frequently at the time. It could be applied quickly and easily on anyone, regardless of the subject's size. Each officer had this hold performed on him on numerous occasions.

During its time, this hold probably saved a lot of lives for officers and suspects. The procedure was banned in the 1980s because of the fear it would break a suspect's neck. What apparently happened was when PCP (a mind altering drug) became popular on the streets it caused its victims to obtain super human strengths; they would resist the hold so fiercely, causing the suspect to break his or her own neck.

Now before the day was over would come the runs. All cadets in formation up and down the hills of Elysian Park. We never knew how long the run would be on any given day—it could be one mile or eight miles, depending upon the mood of the instructor.

One thing about our training officers, they never asked the class or an individual cadet to do anything that they wouldn't do right along-side us. They ran every step with us, up and down the hills, shouting cadence, "LLLAAAPPPDDD, LAPD, LLLAAAPPPDDD, LAPD."

All in all, it was a proud run—officers learned who they were, where they were going and where they came from. Every Los Angeles police officer went through that same hard time, thus creating a brotherhood. Even though there are shortcuts when performing most tasks in life, there were no shortcuts in the LAPD. In other states, training is limited, and doesn't offer know-how or expertise. But in Los Angeles, policemen learned to live together, fight together and stay together. We were truly formed into a single unit. It is with this attitude the department settled for nothing less than the best, striving always to be number one.

How proud a man is to graduate from the academy. My dad traveled from Oklahoma to watch the ceremony, witnessing a parade of honored graduates. Thomas Reddin, my first chief, inspected the troops. Five months of hell ended with a party and gala affair.

For the first time in months, I would have a weekend off, reporting for duty on Monday as an official beat patrol officer with the LAPD, assigned to 77th Division Patrol, p.m. watch.

When the telephone rang on Saturday afternoon, it should have been an indication of the years to come. Holidays, nights, weekends, whenever needed, I would serve the LAPD and the people of Los Angeles, when summoned.

"Can you report for duty," the watch commander's words rang out.

When I reminded him I wasn't scheduled to report until Monday, the lieutenant said, "Damn boy, haven't you seen the TV, we're in the middle of riots at 77th Street. We need every available man."

It was my first taste of life on the streets of Los Angeles, the reality of all this police training would soon set in…angry crowds, violence, hatred for policemen, it was all there the night this boy from Afton reported for the first official assignment in the City of Angels.

It appeared that all of Watts was burning again similar to the Watts Riots of 1965. The weekend began with a Watts Festival which was a carnival-like atmosphere celebrating the anniversary of the Watts Riots that occurred three years earlier. With the weather hot, tempers flared as hooligans and troublemakers, usually not part of the community, filled the streets, and what came to be known as the mini-riots of 1968 was well underway.

We were assigned four officers to a car, all armed with shotguns. I saw every Ma and Paw store on the streets of the Watts district had been hit by Molotov cocktails. Being fired upon from a distance by angry throngs of people throwing debris at police, it proved to be one of the scariest days of my career.

There were hundreds of people looting stores, running every direction in the night, carrying TVs, clothing, and anything else they could steal. The smell of smoke and gunpowder, sweat and fear, and the sound of people crying rang out into the night. Others just roamed the streets in packs, threatening anyone who would dare be in their way.

While stopped at a stoplight an oncoming car nearly hit the patrol car that I was a passenger in. Then it veered to the right and came to rest inches from our police vehicle, making it impossible to open the driver or left passenger doors of the police vehicle. I was seated in the back right rear of the police vehicle. I saw the young male driver of that vehicle immediately duck down out of sight. My first reaction was to bail out of the car, running around the patrol car and the suspect car and placing my shotgun in the driver's side window, waiting for the male to rise again, in full belief when he did, he would be coming up with a gun in his hand.

But when the scared youth raised back up, he was screaming, "My brake pedal stuck on the floor and I was trying to pull it back up."

This young man will never know how close he came to being a statistic. Thank God I didn't do something stupid and ruin my life by shooting him. I had the patience to wait and see if he had a gun and didn't just fire out of instinct. The young man was sent on his way.

With only an instant to make a decision, during the course of duty a bad decision can be construed by the public with a demand for punishment, ostracizing an officer forever. Within a split second officers had to make life and death decisions that could be hashed over and 'Monday-morning quarterbacked' for years by everyone in the court system.

It was just a tip of the iceberg in terms of days to come. I signed up for the tour, so I couldn't cry about it now.

My graduating class at the Los Angeles Police Academy in May, 1968. I am seated on the first row, far right.

Chapter Two

Watts on Patrol

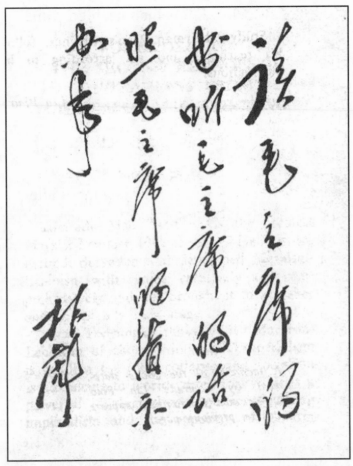

Although none of the Black Panthers were known to possess the ability to read Chinese, this is a sample of the writing of Mao Tse-Tung in 'The Little Red Book' a handbook used by the Black Panthers.

Watts was a 20 square mile section of south Los Angeles. A low income, high crime area, people living in the Watts district fell victim to neighbor disputes, family brawls, burglaries and a variety of other crimes. A predominantly black area, there was only a few elderly Caucasians and Hispanics who had been there for years. Like any other impoverished community, crime was high because many people were out of work and had a lot of idle time on their hands. Drugs, alcohol and prostitution seemed to be on every street corner.

But for the most part, people took care of each other and had a perception of police officers as bad guys. Blacks came to the defense of white people and vice versa. Rioting against authority could occur at any moment and when violence erupted, there was danger to the entire neighborhood.

The civil rights movement was a very prominent issue of the day. Black Panthers, Ron Kringa and the American Communist Party—it seemed as if all these groups wanted to stir the pie. For a time the people in the cities were becoming at war with themselves. We were the thin blue line between the sanity and insanity.

I remember the Black Panther party when it first became a faction formed by Huey Newton and Bobby Seals in Oakland, with some of their more famous members such as Angela Davis and Eldridge Cleaver.

Huey Newton was once tried and convicted for killing a San Francisco police officer. Imprisoned from 1966-67, one of the battle cries of the Black Panthers was 'free Huey Newton.' He was fatally shot during a drug deal gone bad, August 22, 1989, on the streets of San Francisco.

In later years, Angela Davis became a professor at the University of California—Berkley.

Bobby Seals, once accused of killing a police officer and was involved in the Black Panther shooting at 41st and Central in south Los Angeles, in later years ran for city council of Oakland.

Eldridge Cleaver served as the Minister of Information for the Black Panther Party. While imprisoned for rape, he wrote a book, *Soul on Ice*. Several years after his release from prison, he hijacked a plane to Cuba during the late 1960s. Interviewed on television before his death in 1998, Eldridge Cleaver had emerged a model citizen. After going into exile in Algeria in 1968, he returned to the United States, announcing his conversion to Christianity.

But in the late 1960s, the Black Panthers spent their time preaching hatred to the white, and the police in particular, where the slogan "off a pig" was made famous. The Black Panther Party's bible, carried by all members, was Quotations From Chairman Mao Tse-Tung, termed The Little Red Book, containing quotes from the famous communist party leader.

The Black Panthers recruited members from black neighborhoods, serving breakfast to the poor children before school each morning.

Their dress was military green fatigues with black combat boots and if one could be afforded, a black leather jacket and black beret. Little Ma and Pa dry cleaners were real targets for burglars during this period of time, with the main items stolen being black leather jackets customers left to be dry-cleaned.

Black Panthers were always eager to salute with the black power sign, a closed clinched right fist rose high above the head.

The group took credit for several ambushes and murders of police officers in northern California. During several occasions gunfire erupted. Some police officers were wounded, Black Panthers were killed, but never was a Los Angeles police officer killed in the line of duty by a Black Panther in the City of Angels due to

the high quality of training received by all officers.

Once the Black Panthers turned on one of
their own members, Alex Rackley. Suspected of
being disloyal, Rackley was tied to a chair and
tortured for hours. After pouring boiling water
on him, fellow member Warren Kimbro shot
Rackley in the head and his body was found
floating in a river near New Haven, Conneticut.

A few years later, Kimbro, the shooter,
received a scholarship to attend Harvard. He
was later named assistant dean at Eastern Con-
necticut State College.

Erica Huggins, the woman who poured
boiling water on Rackley, was later elected to
serve on a California school board.

These two Black Panthers were fortunate
enough to seek legal counsel from two rising
stars. Bill Lan Lee, now the head of the Civil
Rights division of the U.S. Department of Justice, counseled Black Panthers. As did a second
relatively unknown attorney at the time--the
current democratic candidate for the State of
New York and America's First Lady, Hillary
Rodham Clinton.

In later years, Black Panthers realized
they could get more accomplished by changing
their tactics—instead of waging war in the

streets, they began actively seeking political offices and changing laws.

The Black Panthers was just one of the many obstacles I encountered when p.m. watch began at 4 o'clock in the afternoon. The 77th Street precinct answered many calls of service from people whose lives were literally hanging between the balance of life and death. When people were chasing each other through the projects, screaming and hollering, it was often difficult to apprehend a suspect.

From this experience, I learned three things still practiced today: Presence of command, looking and acting professional, and speaking calmly with common sense, could get the job done. If you're polite and courteous, you can take the queen bee right out of the hive. With good verbal skills you don't have to fight, and I knew I wasn't a big guy. So I fine-tuned the art of verbal communication, a key one in particular was not talking down to people, particularly those who were paying my salary. If they're in the wrong, they know it and officers didn't have to act like a tough guy or bully to get the job done. But you couldn't be too nice either, because some people on the streets associate kindness with being weak.

The patrol always worked in pairs, which

became critical during domestic encounters that usually proved to be most dangerous. Thinking as one and protecting each other became necessary for survival. The only call more dangerous was an unknown trouble call.

Early on in my career, in Long Beach two outstanding police officers answered a call in an upstairs apartment in Seal Beach, where a husband and wife were at odds.

The husband was asked to leave by officers. He requested his jacket from another room and the officers allowed him to leave their sight of vision to retrieve the jacket. He returned with a weapon. The gun battle that ensued ended with both officers, the suspect and his wife dead at the scene. All this in return for one small act of kindness when the suspect requested, "Can I have my coat."

The incident would be one of many that would serve as a lesson to always follow a code taught in the academy—never let a suspect out of your sight.

Later that same year, while off duty, bowling on a league at Cal Bowl in north Long Beach, a gentleman approached me and stated, "Are you a police officer?" When I said yes I work for the Los Angeles Police Department, he spoke "I don't know why I knew, but you look,

act and remind me of my son. His son was a
Long Beach police officer and was one of those
officers killed at the family dispute just mentioned.

I never worked day watch. Evening watch
or morning watch (midnight to 8 a.m.) was a
time for the most dangerous of calls. It was also
where I felt most at home, in the middle of the
action.

The rapid transit bus system in Los Angeles still took money for fares, making a target for
young hoodlums and thugs to rob, although only
small amounts of change could be obtained.

I remember my first arrests while working
with one of the most seasoned training officers,
a well-respected member of the force. During
roll call we received information that at 2 p.m. a
robbery of a RTD bus had occurred at 103rd
Street and Central Avenue. The suspect was a
lone male Negro, black hair, brown eyes, wearing a long black trench coat. The weapon used
was a 12-inch butcher knife. This same suspect
boarded and robbed another bus at the same
location an hour later.

After roll call we drove to the scene and
observed sitting on the bus bench, one male
Negro wearing a black trench coat. Now you
didn't have to be a rocket scientist to want to

visit with this man. During a cursory search for weapons, performed for his safety and ours, I found a 12-inch butcher knife in his waistband and a pocket full of quarters. I had made my first arrest for robbery.

Each day during roll call, each officer would receive a hot sheet listing in numerical order all the stolen cars and "wanted" vehicles (those used in the commission of a crime). The wanted vehicles would be designated with an asterisk, showing it was hot. As we drove from call to call, I checked every car I saw against the hot sheet.

After only about a week on patrol my training officer brought the police vehicle to a stop behind another automobile, stopped at a red light. I looked at the license plate of the vehicle ahead, then at the hot sheet, then back at the license plate again, back to the hot sheet again—not really believing my eyes.

"A stolen car," I screamed so loudly it must have startled my partner.

He asked, "What?"

"A stolen car, in front of us, it's on the hot sheet," I hollered. "Right here, see, it's a sto-len," while pointing to the hot sheet.

I had gotten my first stolen car off of the hot sheet. But from that day forward, I always had a hot sheet with me—it proved to be a valuable tool and I made a game out of it, trying to find a stolen or wanted car.

At the time the prevalence of teen gangs were not as active as found today on the streets of Los Angeles. In those days, officers were trained to handle gangs, and never lost a policeman to urban guerilla warfare because they always backed each other up and never went alone. Of course, gangs were not as active and had a lot less firepower. Most of their weapons were stolen handguns and shotguns, taken by breaking into their neighbors' homes. High-powered rifles were not found because big-game hunting was not a popular sport among the citizens of Watts. Shotguns were the choice of weapon to protect the home; we rarely found automatic weapons. Of course this changed soon enough.

Reflecting on those experiences, I remember everyone worked and enjoyed a rewarding occupation even though it was a seriously dangerous time in history.

I lived in a patrol car, the job became more important than anything. Lupe seemed to understand my love of police work and supported it because she knew I was happy in my chosen field. The pay was good, the best job I

could have found being a man with a high
school education and few college hours. I always believed a good policeman was a young
man who had street smarts, common sense,
loved people, and had a burning desire to be a
policeman.

I was soon to find out a different breed
would be entering the force. In the early 1970s,
the aerospace industry bottomed out and at the
time LAPD officers were making about $25,000
per year. Aerospace people and other white-
collar workers were out of work. Since most had
college degrees, they could read, write and take
tests well. When their profession went belly up,
many became police officers, not because they
wanted to serve the people of the community.
Due to their higher educations, they could easily
pass the sergeant's test with higher scores than
the average street cop. This would enable them
to secure desk jobs (paper shufflers) and rise
through the ranks rapidly.

They didn't know siccum from come
here. There's nothing wrong with getting a
college degree but common sense doesn't come
from the halls of higher education. To know
what is going on, you have to get down in the
trenches a while.

I had worked Watts about 180 days when

I would first question what this Okie was doing in the streets and alleys of Los Angeles.

Things worked fast in Watts. Within six months I had responded to thousands of complaints and made hundreds of arrests. I was proud and cocky, one super cop with the attitude "a bullet can't touch me."

The events that unfolded at 10 p.m. on Valentine's Day would bring me down a notch.

My partner was a young black officer, fresh out of the academy. This would be his first night on the street. Being a rainy Monday night not much excitement was expected so I was the senior officer and training officer with only six months experience on the street myself. We answered numerous radio calls during the early evening where I stressed safety and tried to show my new partner for the evening my expertise in leadership.

At about 9:50 p.m., we received a radio call to a family dispute in progress at 10606 South Central Avenue. There was a light mist falling as I parked on Central in front of this location. Noting that this was an apartment building, I asked the dispatcher for further information, inquiring the specific unit number. This apartment building was a two story complex facing north onto an open parking lot, Central being on the west side and an alley running behind the building to the east.

There were three apartments downstairs and three upstairs, each having a large picture window and a door. As I waited word from the dispatcher for the unit number, I observed a black and white pull into the alley and the officers began speaking with a male suspect. Thinking that they had the male half of my family dispute I exited the police vehicle, my partner close behind and walked directly across the parking lot toward this black and white.

As I approached their location a lady came from one of the downstairs apartments and stated, "I'm the one that called the police and they're upstairs in number six."

I quickly walked to the west staircase, followed by another officer, not being my partner, but the passenger officer from the black and white. This officer had just transferred into 77th division from juvenile division three days prior. As I approached a picture window with the drapes pulled revealing only a dim light inside, I whispered to the other officer, "I don't see any movement inside," as I peered between the drapes and window sill. What I didn't realize, I was looking into the wrong apartment.

Then I heard a door crack open and immediately turned my attention to the direction of the sound and saw a male Negro peering through a four-inch crack in the doorway, the door opened inward toward his face. I took a step toward him and stated, "Did you call the police?"

What I didn't know at that time, was after I left the patrol car down below in the alley, the woman had further stated, "That guy in number six has a gun and will kill a policeman." Unknown to me at the time, those two officers immediately started running up the east stairway in my direction, but it was too late.

As I spoke to the gentleman peering out at me I saw his hand go to his waistband, in a flash withdrawing what appeared to be a blue steel .38 caliber revolver. Now I saw fire fly and heard glass breaking. I never heard shots fired by anyone, but realizing I was under fire from four feet away, I immediately dropped to the floor in a prone position, returning fire on the way down. I must have smelled trouble, for I had already un-holstered my weapon and was carrying it in my right hand, hidden behind my right leg.

The officers coming up the east stairway toward me were also firing in my direction. The door slammed shut and silence prevailed. Yes it was just like the movies, flames from the muzzle blast looked like cannon fire. It all appeared to be in slow motion.

I scrambled back down the steps to safety. Once at the steps, I realized that my fellow officer was down. The other officers raced down the steps toward the police car screaming on the radio, "Officer needs help, shots fired, officer down."

A young sergeant who had arrived at the location just as I had started for the stairs soon met me. He asked who the fallen officer was. I told him I didn't know, but we were going to get him now. The sergeant said he realized I was hurt but not to worry the ambulance was on its way. I assured him I didn't need an ambulance but the other officer did.

The sergeant and myself dragged the fallen officer to safety, all the time not knowing if that door was going to fly open, the suspect re-appear and fire again. As we dragged the fallen officer to safety, placing him into an ambulance to be taken to the hospital, the bond was instantaneous.

The young sergeant told me another ambulance was en route and would be there shortly for me. I wanted to know what for because I hadn't been hit. "Sometimes it doesn't hurt right away," he told me, "but we want to get you checked out."

I finally convinced him that I hadn't been shot. During the brief gun battle the plate glass window had fallen on my back but I didn't even receive a cut. It was hard to believe that all these rounds had been fired in my direction and I wasn't hit but an officer behind me was. It was just not my day to go end of watch.

When the sergeant and I entered the apartment where the suspect had fired from, the shooter's body was discovered, one shot through the heart. He had fired six rounds and even after being fatally wounded, slumped to the arm of a couch and had ejected all six spent rounds, attempting to re-load, when he finally fell to the floor and expired at 10:05 p.m.

An investigation revealed this suspect had been guilty of a few liquor store robberies during the past month. After drinking all day and taking drugs, he began arguing with his wife. Since she wasn't the one that called the police, when he saw me walking to his door, the suspect presumed that I was coming after him for robbery. He got his gun, telling his wife, "they're coming after me but I won't go alive."

The fallen officer had a flashlight in his left hand, gun in his right hand at the time of the shooting. He never saw the suspect and never knew anyone was around until the shooting began. He hadn't heard the door crack open, nor did he see the gun come up from the waistband. As I went down it left this officer exposed. His immediate reaction was to throw his flashlight hand up in front of his face where one bullet went through his hand, lodging inside the flash-light battery. Spinning him around to his left, the second bullet hit him in the gun belt just above the empty holster, lodging near his spine. He recovered but the bullet remains in him to this day.

Around 4 a.m. the condition of my fellow officer unknown, I was escorted back to the scene for completion of the investigation re-ports. As we were walking through the scene, I saw rats crawling out of the trashcans, making me realize I was a long way from home.

The evening of the shooting I formed a bond that will never be broken with the young sergeant that came to my aid at the scene. I have since worked for him as a sergeant in patrol, a sergeant in vice, a lieutenant on the SWAT team and the captain of metro division. He has since retired and has become the chief of police in a major southern California city. I am proud to have served with this fine gentleman.

Years later during a SWAT mission, this sergeant asked, "Okie we have worked together so long and been through so much, I'm embarrassed to tell you but Okie is the only name I know you by. What is your real first name anyway?"

The next evening during roll call, officers congratulated me on a job well done. I had reacted to my training and it was at that moment I became one of them. I had followed the code to the letter and didn't get hurt in the process— my training had saved my life as it would many times over. There was no celebration over the injury of one of our own. All of the atta boys were part of the bond of brotherhood. Only police officers know what each other faces. These offers of congratulations were not for the taking of a life, which it may appear, if an outsider were to see it. It was explained to me later on in my career that sometimes we laugh and appear to be having fun in times of grief and stress; it's the brain's way to keep one sane. On smaller forces officers aren't as close as in large cities where training shortcuts are never used.

Back in those days an officer didn't get relieved of street duties until the incident was determined a justified shooting.

After roll call that same day, my first

radio call was a family dispute in progress at 89th and San Pedro Streets. As I pulled to the curb I have to say that the events of the night before were heavily on my mind. It was hard to get out of that patrol car and walk up to that door. It was about this time three black and whites pulled up, the officers exited and said, "Come on Okie, let's do this one together." It was a way to get back on the horse that just threw me. Those officers knew full well how it would be. Thanks guys, wherever you are today.

Several weeks later, the coroner's inquest revealed the dead man was originally from Oklahoma with a long background of scrapes with the law. It took a jury of six only ten minutes to review the information and clear my fellow officers and I of any wrongdoing.

During a jury deliberation, the victim's identical twin brother approached me in the hallway. It was both eerie and frightening as he looked exactly like the man we were just discussing on the witness stand. The twin wanted the gun returned since he was the original owner.

It would be only one of many events during my career that I was thrust into emotionally charged domestic situations where I didn't particularly care to be.

The first Christmas on patrol was the
most difficult to keep my emotions in check—
and has proved to be such a haunting experience
that bitter memories of that holiday season are
forever etched in my mind.

It was early Christmas evening around
dark, when I was summoned to a family dispute.
Pulling up in front of a home of a Hispanic
family, I remember seeing a shattered picture
window. About 20 family members were all
embroiled in a bitter confrontation. The son had
beaten his father severely then tossed the Christmas tree through the front glass where it lay in
the yard.

But nothing compared to what I would
find at 11:30 that same evening on 87th street,
when the dispatcher signaled an officer needed
help, shots fired. Arriving at the location, I was
met by two police officers I knew had been
involved in the shooting. Another man was lying
on the front steps, bleeding profusely onto the
sidewalk. It was a chilly night and steam rose
from the scarlet pool of blood.

As I stepped into the house, I saw one of
the most horrifying sights I have ever witnessed.
Two children about three and four years old,
looked like bunny rabbits on the couch, but it
was an optical illusion because the mind would

not allow the horror to register. As I moved closer, the fluffy cotton was the stuffing from the old couch and its maroon color was in reality, blood from the fatal shotgun blasts inflicted on the children.

The man responsible for the shooting was dead on the front steps. His estranged wife was in the hospital giving birth to the couple's third child. The mother-in-law, taking care of the children while her daughter was giving birth, became involved in a dispute with her son-in-law and he tossed her out of the house. She ran next door and called the police. He shot his babies just as the police arrived at the scene and officers returned fire at the doorstep, too late to save the children.

The holiday season always seemed to be a time when domestic abuse peaked and the cruelties of living in Watts became a stark reality. It never changed throughout the 20 years of my law enforcement career—something tragic always reared its ugly head during the holidays.

This was the beginning of my down right hatred for the festivities. At this time of year hard-working, good, honest people can do crazy things like rob stores, sell drugs, or themselves, to buy toys for their kids.

Not all evil things were saved until after

sundown. In 1970, just two years after my academy class went out on the street to become part of that thin blue line, my classmate, Officer Earl Riddick, a young black officer with a family, gave the ultimate price for his act of pure heroism.

While off-duty and in a bank conducting personal business, a lone male robbed the bank. Officer Riddick, observing this and knowing full well what the outcome could possibly be, followed the suspect outside to the parking lot for the protection of citizens. He identified himself as a police officer and tried to place the suspect under arrest. A gun battle ensued and Officer Riddick was fatally wounded. The suspect was later found and killed by officers in another gun battle.

Officer Riddick's son carries on his father's proud tradition by serving as a police officer for the City of Angels.

Nobody, not even family nor friends, would ever know exactly how ugly things were on the streets during those first two years. But despite the horror, I loved living a little boy's dream and truly wanted to help people. After all, somebody had to do it.

If people knew what the streets were really like, they'd never turn the lights off at night.

Chapter Three

Undercover Operations

Two years and numerous commendations later, I was recognized for outstanding duties as a uniformed police officer and offered a very good promotion to 77th division's vice squad— going undercover.

Unlike the movies and television stories, the vice squad does not deal in narcotics, murders, rapes or such crimes and there is very little glamour. It was fun time that included roll playing every night and acting like anyone you ever dreamed to be.

Busting up prostitution and gambling rings was the name of the game and partners became crafty at devising plans to watch operations while going unnoticed.

Less glamorous of my duties was alcoholic beverage control, commonly known in Los Angeles as ABC checks. Any establishment with a liquor license cannot refuse to be checked for infractions of the law by any peace officer in the State of California.

One of the biggest crimes people don't usually associate with liquor laws is watering down booze. Many bars would sell good whiskey for $4 a drink, which netted a profit on 32 ounces per fifth. To stretch a dollar, extending a profit considerably, bartenders would pour a quarter of a fifth of whiskey into another container, refilling that portion with water. The resulting product sold at 50 ounces a fifth instead of the legal 32 ounces. The unsuspecting patron would never know they had just been had.

Officers had the right to inspect back storerooms and during many unexpected visits, would discover cases of booze in the process of being watered down. It was always a good sign when you saw a case of 12 bottles opened, with a funnel sticking out of one of the bottles. This happened on many occasions.

Another infraction of the law is commonly called substitutions. This is where a patron asks for a particular brand of drink such as Crown Royal and is served a cheaper brand in its place.

The easiest way to catch bartenders in this practice was for undercover officers to pose as drunks, dressed up in Sunday go to meetin' clothes one day and like Skid Row bums the next. With a partner seated at each end of the bar, they each began ordering drinks. Serving the first drink called for, the bartender would pull out the requested brand.

After a few drinks, and seemingly not paying attention, ordering the same high dollar brand, the bartender would usually pour well whiskey (lesser priced house bourbon) instead of the specific call drink. When people are intoxicated their taste buds are inhibited and sometimes they were served a house drink at premium price.

Often times, an establishment only held a beer license, so it was another offense to sell the whiskey, or have it on the premises, be it premium or not, to any patron. Then there were always the good old boys who had no license at all.

Serving drinks after-hours was another infraction we worked often. All bars and night-clubs had to stop serving at 2 a.m.

Officers would drive the streets and if they saw more cars than usual around the night-club or bar after hours, it was a sure sign drinks were being served.

If you knocked on the door and tried to get in, if they opened the door at all, which wasn't probable, drinks would be poured out destroying the evidence before you could get through the door. So it was always a challenge and a new game to play on how to get inside before the evidence went down the drain.

One method that always worked because of human nature, officers would stack several empty trashcans on the sidewalk in front of the bar.

Another officer drove the police car down the street at a high rate of speed, slamming on the brakes. Two or three other officers would throw the cans creating, causing a ruckus of crashing tin and squealing brakes that sounded like an accident had just occurred. The doors of the bar would fly open with all the patrons running out to see if their cars had been hit by another drunk.

The officers would step in behind them and find an easy path to the bar where drinks were being served.

Other times it was as simple as waiting for the doors to open and casually invite ourselves in for a drink.

The patrons were never arrested. The bartenders and barmaids would be cited for serving after hours. With about two citations, the establishment could lose their liquor license.

This work was always done between 2 a.m. and six a.m.

Lupe describes this phase of her husband's career as, "a good time running around with a bunch of guys."

I remember one time coming home after I'd been working all night and Lupe wanted the yard looking good before company arrived later in the evening.

"You need to get that lawn mowed to-day," she said.

"I'm tired, I worked all night," I told her.

"You didn't work, you ran around drinking and gambling all night with a bunch of guys. Now today you're going to mow the lawn," she replied.

What could I say? Our guests were greeted with freshly cut grass.

Chapter Four

Prostitution

Prostitution never seemed too appealing to me, especially after the great adventure of arresting streetwalkers in Watts.

There were no houses of ill repute in Watts, per say, because pimps robbed them taking a pretty hefty percentage, causing most to freelance their service. The majority of streetwalkers were independent business people. The episodes on television portraying pimps are simply unfounded; normally they provide some sort of protection to the ladies, but for a price.

It seemed to be a no-morals situation. You can't have morals and sell your body. But ours is not to judge because when your babies are crying, there are a lot of things we might all do when our kids are hungry.

Most were victims of family violence and hooked on some form of narcotics—heroin being the drug of choice back in those days. Marijuana was a favorite, but cocaine was too expensive at the time. Crank, ice or PCP was unheard of in those days.

Many carried sexually transmitted diseases, however AIDS was an unheard of disease at this time. Many were lesbians or bisexual, with no moral character and drawn to the lowest form of nature. Most were forced into prostitution because they had babies or drug habits to support.

But when you talk to them in private, in the dark of the night, they are sad, to be pitied. They all began with the same hopes and dreams everyone else did. Who knows what went wrong. Girls had their own story to tell—some continually looked for the rich man coming to sweep them off their feet and carry them away forever. Others said they were saving their money for school and would someday be somebody—only they would know in their dreams. Most had just been dealt a bad hand from the beginning and never dared let their dreams be known. Many girls just ran away from a traumatic past and things never got any better.

I tried to make it as comfortable as possible while arresting and transporting them, because they had a bad lot in life as it was.

The ladies of the evening called themselves "sporting ladies." They walked facing traffic, waving at lone males. If the practice is allowed to run into residential neighborhoods, wives can't even go to the store to get a loaf of bread without a guy trying to pick her up and young girls can't walk home from school without someone propositioning them.

But it doesn't take long to become an

expert at spotting prostitutes. I can tell if a girl is working the streets by the way she carries herself and the way she walks. But then so could the tricks or the johns, so that is no great feat.

Dressing up as a factory worker, construction hand or a variety of other potential occupations, it became one of the most fun jobs because every day was different. The undercover attire could be of any form with the exception of two occupations—that of a clergyman and a journalist. Those two fields are strictly off limits because training mandated that we never lose faith in the press or religion, two professions where livelihood depends on the utmost in confidence and trust.

One way we arrested prostitutes was letting your partner out of the vehicle and then drive by the lady working the street. While my partner watched from a point of concealment, she would flag me down and make an offer of sex for money. This could include various sex acts, the price ranging from $10 to $50, depending on what the customer wanted.

"What are you doing tonight," she would say, adding, "You're not the police are you?"

"Just driving around, thought you might need a ride," I would reply.

The girl would usually ask, "Do you want

a date." 'Date' referred to having a sex act.

"I don't know what you mean," I would state.

"How much money you got baby," she would ask, adding, "Now don't take all night to shop."

"Oh I don't know how much does it cost," I asked.

Then she would say, "Head $10, half and half is $30, or a straight lay is $20."

At which time I would always ask, "Where do we go, to a hotel room?"

Sometimes afraid of being robbed, the girl would say, "Don't worry baby, I'll give it to you in the car."

Other times she would say she had a room close by and tell me to just follow her.

The dialog was nearly the same each time as the streetwalker stuck her head into the car.

After the deal was made I would signal my partner and an arrest was made.

An officer can't make an offer of money or he would be soliciting and then entrapment exists. When operating a girl, I spoke as if I were a customer, or John as they are called.

One amazing realization was the professions of men who solicited and became clients of the Watts prostitutes. There were doctors, lawyers, and people of great power and wealth seeking the services of a streetwalker. I would see guys from all walks of life; it could be the man next door.

It wasn't exactly what anyone would call a high-class business and couldn't be good for anyone. Ninety percent of the girls gave head because they wouldn't get the clap. It was a short time, wham, bam, thank you ma'am with little time required so the girls could get back to the street and open for business again. They wore no underclothes because the less a working girl had on the quicker the deed was done. Taking off clothes and making idle conversation take time and time was money.

To catch the clients engaging in the search for a prostitute, officers would observe a man stop for a brief chat with one of the ladies. A working girl always gets the money first, so conversation takes place, and then the couple drove into the shadows of an alley. Usually the pair was arrested for lewd acts in public, which is a more serious crime than prostitution because passersby can observe the act.

Some work out of a hotel room and can be followed to the exact location. Motel operators charge by the hour if working with prostitutes and the operators of these establishments were well known to police. Many of the women were arrested over a dozen times each, most were found occupying the same room time after time.

Listening at the motel room door, the same conversation always takes place. And it's not an all-night affair. Once the couple starts to haggle over the price, an arrest can be made.

The motel manager provided a master key when entry was requested because he valued door jams. After about the third time of replacing the door jams, he gladly gave the room key to police.

Prostitution among the gay community was the most difficult to deal with. I hated to work gay males because many people who witnessed undercover officers talking to gay males naturally assumed a love interest was apparent. Posing in the gay community was an unnatural act for many officers and a job detested by most.

During the late 1960s and early 1970s, gays were discriminated against and it was a dangerous deed to arrest a family man who might lose his position in life. The drag queens were not socially accepted at the time and were working as girls; there were many men who solicited these prostitutes without knowing they were males in drag. That's what the tricks would all claim when arrested, but it just can't be.

This was back before all of the operations and hormone drugs that can enlarge breasts and can take away beards. It's hard to imagine you're with a woman when she has a five o'clock shadow and smelly socks stuffed into a dirty bra for breasts. Now I'm an Okie from the sticks and I could spot them from a mile away but there was always the exception who really did appear to be a female—I have been fooled, but then I wasn't cheek to cheek either.

They also had the strength of a man and the emotion of a woman—sometimes a deadly combination.

At a restaurant at Western and Manchester Street, a well-endowed female with size 14 feet, large Adam's apple and hands big enough to cover a basketball was being arrested for prostitution.

Our sergeants, a supervisor in charge of vice squad, had not been on the streets much, but wanted to make the arrest. My partner and I didn't tell our superior the prostitute was not a girl.

The sergeant let the drag queen get in the car with him and the minute he identified himself as a police officer and advised her she was under arrest, she promptly smacked him in the arm with a tire tool.

I immediately took the tire tool away from the prostitute, by reaching it from an open back window. This sergeant, being the one I spoke earlier of becoming a lifelong friend. Standing 6 foot 6 and weighing 220 pounds, complete with a bodybuilder's frame, he resembled Mr. Clean. To this day, I still tease him about saving him from being beaten to death by a drag queen.

Another mistaken identity occurred after a beautiful young lady wearing a mink coat was arrested. At the time I thought I was experienced at spotting the drag queens. This suspect was so nice she put up no fight during the arrest.

En route to the station, I asked why, when she appeared to have so much class, was she working the streets. The lady just cooed, giggled and made eyes all the way to jail.

But when the pretty young lady was put into the holding tank, to my horror, I realized my mistake as the other female prisoners began yelling, "You put a guy in here."

To which the beautiful woman known as Sharon, stepped forward and identified himself as a local drag queen, "It's me Officer Myers."

From that day on, Sharon made a very good snitch, calling to let me know when things were going down on the streets. So much so that Lupe began to recognize Sharon's voice on the telephone. Being nice to the drag queen paid off despite how embarrassing the situation was at the time.

Human nature is funny—people rarely look upward, therefore watching prostitutes from above gave an insight to many things on the streets below. The flat rooftop of a garage on the corner of Western Street provided a favorite lookout. The working girls would look up and down the streets for any sign of the police and I could hear them say, "I wonder where the hell Officer Myers is? He's always lurking around here somewhere." They failed to look up, never seeing the undercover officers watching from above and hearing every word they said.

Another favorite overhead lookout was a two-story building located at the corner of Slauson and Broadway Streets. It was here that my brother Ned, a man who had never ventured out of Oklahoma, found entertainment of a lifetime.

Ned had been diagnosed with terminal cancer when he and his wife came to visit Lupe and I in California. He wanted to see what I did during undercover sting operations so my partner and I took Ned along, and headed out for an evening of working prostitutes.

Sitting atop of the tall building, with our feet dangling over the edge, Ned watched in amazement as my partner called to officers standing by.

"Pick up the girl in the red dress...purple dress," we radioed to officers below who in turn loaded up the girls and hauled them to the station.

But it was one blatant act that left Ned in stitches. One big-butted girl wearing a thigh-high black dress, obviously stoned, stepped out into the middle of the street, pulling her dress up to show her wares, waving and hollering at all the oncoming cars.

"Hey white boy, pussy, ten dollars," she screamed pointing to her crotch.

Ned began laughing so hard he almost fell off the roof, blowing our cover. His laughter became contagious and even the working girls that overheard us, looked above for once during the evening, breaking out in a chorus of laughter as well.

Another episode working prostitution literally tickled my funny bone, to the point that it almost landed me jail time for contempt of court.

The vice squad received a complaint of a prostitute working the area of Broadway and 77th Streets, an unusual corner since the police station was located at that intersection. A neighborhood bar-b-cue, Hoggly Woggly's, was located on nearby Florence Avenue.

A quick assessment of the situation revealed a Negro lady, in her 50s, uglier than a boot, waving at lone male drivers as they passed by. The scene had every sign of prostitution and when I dropped off my partner, she flagged me over, immediately proceeding to violate sex for sale ordinances. The partner is signaled and an arrest was made.

This woman was distraught, not a typical streetwalker. She had hungry babies at home and was trying to make money to live. It was a sad situation that nobody likes to be placed in.

In court, a jury trial began with a public defender working on the woman's behalf. After I recounted how I observed the violations, the accused took the stand, adamantly denying all guilt.

"Man I was not whoring," she stated staunchly. "I was only going to Hoggly Woggly's."

The judge looked up, the jury looked up, and the judge asked, "Where?"

She once again replied, "Hoggly Woggly's. You know, Hoggly Woggly's, to get me some barbeque."

For some reason, the statement struck my funny bone and I burst in to gales of uncontrollable laughter during open court.

The defense attorney didn't find my outburst the least bit funny. Nor did the judge see any humor in the statement (that he let on to members of the court room anyway) and ordered me out of the courtroom until I could maintain composure.

Outside, I tried everything in my power and finally managed to straighten myself before returning to the courtroom.

But the minute I entered the courtroom and looked at the defendant, I burst into laughter and had to leave again. I came very close to spending a night in jail for contempt of court.

Working prostitution often led to other crimes in progress. One such evening, my partner and I saw a prostitute get into a car with a trick where they drove to a nearby motel.

I parked in the alley behind the motel and was watching to see which room they entered.

A man came out of a top room, peers

over and stated, "You guys are going to rip this place off, aren't you. They got some nice TVs, let me help you."

"We need some dope," I told the subject.

"I can get you all the dope you want," the dealer replied. "Let me get in the car with you."

"We stole this car," I replied. "Let us dump this one and steal another that won't be reported yet."

The man agreed and officers sped to the station to trade the car for another with a radio in the glove box.

Picking up our newfound drug connection a few minutes later, he led us to a house located near an alley, just west of Figueroa and 75th Street.

"I'm down from San Francisco, and my cousin lives here," he told us.

He left the car and went inside, returning a few moments later with an irate man wanting to know who we were and what the hell we wanted.

I told him we came down from San Francisco and wanted to buy marijuana and gloated that his cousin and I had been friends forever.

My new friends returned into the house, reappearing in a few moments with a half brick of marijuana, wanting only $500 for the merchandise.

Everybody was mad as hell when I announced, "Gotcha."

For a time the newcomer from San Francisco sat sullen in the back of the car. Just needing to have the last word, he retorted, "You guys didn't fool me. I knew all along you were cops."

At this, the cousin stated, "Why don't you shut the fuck up man."

White businessmen were the most dangerous to arrest.

They did not want to lose their position in life and families and would fight to get out of the situation. Many carry guns or knives when entering a seedy part of town. The same goes with gays. In those days gays were still in the closet and weren't recognized as part of our community. When arrested, they would sometimes fight to the death in order to save their reputations.

One evening my partner and I observed two other vice squad team members sneaking into a courtyard of a motel at 78th and Figueroa Streets, so we turned around at the next corner and headed back to see if we could offer assistance. When we arrived on the scene, the two vice officers were leading a young, black man toward us and asked if we would keep him from alerting the prostitutes in one of the rooms of their presence.

Assuming incorrectly that a cursory search for weapons had already been performed, I watched this suspect become very nervous.

"Pat him down, he acts awful strange," I told my partner.

My partner stepped behind the suspect to do as I'd asked, at which time the man pulled a .38 revolver from his waistband and stated, "I have a gun."

My first reaction was to grab this gun as I heard the hammer fall. For some unknown reason, one of the six chambers was empty while the others held cartridges. Thankfully the hammer fell on that empty chamber, and no shots rang out.

I received a letter from Mayor Sam Yorty, a highly respected civic leader among police officers in Los Angeles. "Tell Officer Myers he played a grim game of Russian roulette. I'm glad he won," the letter read. It was one of those rewarding moments when I was glad the mayor took the time and thought enough to tell me thanks. In my opinion he was the last mayor of Los Angeles that truly cared what happened to the police officers within his city.

Then there were some prostitutes who became so baffled in a predicament that they turned themselves in.

One such streetwalker working in front of a motel on Broadway, jumped into an old battered Volkswagen I frequently used in undercover work. I didn't have time to say anything to the woman she just hopped into the car and made a proposition.

When the signal was made and my partner appeared threatening arrest for prostitution I asked him, "What the hell are you doing officer? Look, this is my wife. My attorney will have your ass for this."

The streetwalker played along with it, finishing my sentences of explanation. That is until we arrived upstairs at the vice squad office and a fellow officer looked at me and remarked, "That guy sure looks familiar. Isn't he the guy wanted for bank robbery?"

"You're under arrest for bank robbery," another officer chided. "Cop out and tell me who drove the getaway car."

At this time I said, "Okay, you've got the goods on me. She drove it."

She jumped right off the bench and began screaming, "Officer I'm a whore. You know

I'm a whore and he's a trick."

When my comrades remained undaunted she wailed, "I don't know this man. Take me to jail, I'm a whore."

She got her wish and was immediately processed on charges of solicitation for sex.

On one occasion, my partner and I were in a bar located near 79th and Western Streets, playing pool and trying to work some new girls in town.

We had been at this location nearly two hours when a well-known prostitute came in and walked up to me and said with urgency in her voice, "I need to talk with you."

I told her to meet me in the hallway in the back of the bar near the restrooms and pay phones. She seemed quite concerned and told me that there was a car parked behind our un-marked police vehicle containing four male Negroes. She was afraid for the safety of my partner and myself for it appeared to her they were waiting for us to exit the bar. She felt that maybe we would be the prey for an intended robbery.

I took her advice and used the phone to call for backup, explaining the situation to my watch commander.

Officers were dispatched to my location

and the suspects detained. During a search of the vehicle, they found automatic weapons and two live hand grenades. These suspects were later confirmed to be Black Panthers from the Oakland area.

All in all, knowing the prostitutes and their habits paid off.

When it came down to making the arrest, girls would all act differently, but almost always each girl would do identical things. Some would run down the street hollering "rape, rape," hoping to draw citizens to her rescue. Others would stand and fight, some with knives, hatpins, pencils, anything to hurt you with but that wouldn't be considered a concealed weapon. They carried these items not with sole intent to harm police officers but for the mere protection from some tricks.

Generally when they were high they loved a policeman, most of them knew it was a form of protection. They loved us to be on the street, they just didn't want to go to jail.

But the "hype" as addicts to heroin was termed, revealed the darkest side of prostitution—festered boils from dirty needles were commonplace. Most people who have seen that side of prostitution wouldn't ever be tempted to venture further into that realm. These girls or guys, which ever the case may be, would not stop at anything for a fix, robbing, assault with a deadly weapon, or even murder.

Probably the most intriguing sight I ever witnessed was a slave auction. It was the damnedest thing I'd ever seen at the time.

Young boys, with dark complexions were sold to people practicing sex acts of bondage and slavery. Shackled in chains with piercings galore and adorned in leather, the boys could be led onto a stage where they were auctioned and purchased for $400 to $500 each.

A dungeon below the bar featured a stockade with devices to hold the head and arms still while the men who purchased these slaves could act out their sexual fantasies.

Lupe said working prostitution made me sick in the head, because to this day, I can observe people passing by and just by the way a person carries himself or herself, and I can tell if I'm staring into the eyes of a streetwalker.

In a nutshell, working prostitution was a pretty grotesque job. It certainly was not an occupation that a person would go to Sunday school and visit about the week's activities.

Chapter Five

The Love Children

Intelligence work was a big part of the vice squad mission during the 1970s, infiltrating the hippy segment of the population to find out what the next move might be.

There was unrest at all the college campuses in and around Los Angeles. We would mingle amongst the crowds demonstrating against the Vietnam War or whatever issues the students might be addressing that day. Wherever these demonstrators gathered, sooner or later rock-throwing malay would ensue. It was my job to mingle and report any hot spots or people in the process of agitating the crowds, both for the safety of citizens and police officers alike.

I remember the flower children, as they were called in that day, were always eager to give everyone they came in contact with flowers, hugs and kisses. I received all three of these gifts on many occasions—it was just a way of life. As a general rule, hippies and flower children were a fun-loving group of people trying to find their place in life.

Any chance for a gathering and a good time would be termed a festival and promoters worked overtime at the task of booking bands for entertainment as well as vendors to sell water pipes and any other type of narcotic paraphernalia, incense, black lights and an array of items that were legal to possess at the time.

One such event, the Moon Rock Festival, was held April 3, 1970 in Ascot Park, a place that was normally used as a small racecar track.

Weaving in and out of the park, I saw hundreds of tents hippies had pitched, mostly made from white sheets, designed for relief from the sun.

From these tents, they also opened shops to sell their wares. This could be anything to make a dollar, sandals, rugs, t-shirts, psychedelic pictures with the latest slogans, and of course sometimes drugs, bongs, pipes and paraphernalia. It was one big supermarket and swap meet combined.

With psychedelic music so loud you couldn't hear your own thoughts, the smell of marijuana hanging thick in the air, vice squad members mingled with the love children of the day.

These festivals were a test of how well the officers could disengage themselves from a crowd without getting their ass kicked. It was a lesson in emotion control and cool actions.

Ten officers were assigned to work this crowd of approximately 1,000. One officer among us saw several hippies sitting around a blanket Indian style, all smoking pot with bags of marijuana piled in the center of the blanket.

Our task was merely an intelligence-gathering mission but this officer could not resist, the temptation was too great as he stated, "Police officer, you're under arrest." The officer was immediately jumped on by what must have seemed like hundreds of people.

The call, officer needs help, went out and as officers arrived at the scene, running through the park, chasing suspects. It looked like the Calvary at Little Big Horn—people were running through makeshift sheet tents, in one side and out the other with officers in hot pursuit. Sheets and tent posts were flying through the air. In a matter of 20 minutes there were approximately 20 arrests and the park was empty.

The aftermath resembled an abandoned refugee camp.

With all this excitement there was only one injury to an officer, the original arresting officer, his nose was broken from a kick when he first initiated the action.

Chapter Six

Gambling

In between working the hippy festivals
and the daily routine of prostitution control, my
most serious pastime became mingling amongst
gamblers.

We didn't bother the little old ladies
playing bingo at the church, or people engaged
in a friendly round of pitch or pinochle. We
investigated gambling only when three "C's" of
gambling came into play—commercial, conspicuous or complained of. Commercial gambling is when someone is taking a portion of the
pot; conspicuous is gambling in plain sight
down on the street corner; and complained of is
when the wife calls and says her husband is
spending his entire paycheck betting at the local
bar.

I became an expert in the field of gambling—a field that had seldom been worked in
the City of Los Angeles. A "rare expertise" was
how the department heads described my skill in
dice and cards.

It was a learning experience, figuring out
how people were cheated, and knowing 36
combinations on dice. There are many different
forms of creating dice that give the advantage to
the dishonest person.

A skilled player learned to look carefully
at dice. Some could be a little flatter on the ace

six sides, kind of like a pack of cigarettes. When the dice are thrown, odds are they land on the flatter sides, creating a seven more often than not.

Of course, everyone has heard of loaded dice, where a certain side of the dice is made heavier than the other sides. This will cause the dice to land on one side more than the calculated risk.

Another form of creating a dishonest die would be to round off one corner, called shaved dice. This will also cause the dice to land on one side more often than the others.

I soon became the only qualified gambling expert for the City of Los Angeles, living amongst gamblers for about a year. I taught other officers, my vice unit as well as the citywide vice squad, how to gamble and how to detect dishonest play. The same advice passed on to me from people on the streets.

The gambling aspect became quite a tool. People caught in a dishonest gambling game were arrested for burglary, because the way California statutes are interpreted, anyone who enters a building to commit larceny is guilty of burglary, a felony. A dishonest gambler going into a location with the intent to cheat is in fact committing larceny, so therefore he can be arrested for a felony burglary charge instead of a weak misdemeanor of gambling that would carry only a $25 fine.

I had to know the gambling vernacular because sometimes I wouldn't be able to be inside the location where gambling was taking place, but I could testify to the conversations I heard that revealed gambling was indeed occurring.

While shooting dice gamblers would be hollering and drinking, often times the players didn't pay attention to who came by the door. The shouts of "buy baby a new pair of shoes" and "seven come eleven" or "give me an eight the hard way" and "you're faded" or "let 'em roll" were giveaways.

Nearly 100 cars lined up outside of a house also signaled one hell of a party and quite a large gambling game in progress.

All of the statements would be street jargon that I had to know and translate in a court of law to prove my case.

Sometimes these arrests were made by not actually ever seeing a game. Because we were white, and anybody white was assumed to be the police, the gamblers simply refused to let us enter. In those cases, officers found different ways to listen outside the house. Through the heat ducts, using a stethoscope, the familiar lingo "who's gonna fade me", "okay you're faded," "seven you're a winner," would ring out into the night. "Fading" is covering a bet, and any reasonable man assumes gambling is taking place so the arrest can be made.

If a doorman appeared, he was instructed not to warn people what was coming down. Two officers would arrest enough people to fill a school bus at any one game. These people were usually lined up along the walls and cursory searched for officers' safety. A search of the house would produce guns, brass knuckles, knives, or a trash can full of pot.

It was a cycle and a routine they all knew—get arrested, pay the fine and go back to the next game the next day. Yet it could always pose a risk and I never allowed another officer to take my place—the one time I did, an officer ended up getting shot. Arresting gamblers was a matter of treating people with respect.

Several spots were hit once a week. Each entrepreneur would snitch out the others in an effort to stifle the competition. Everybody told everybody else about the various operations about town.

All in all, gamblers were a bunch of nice guys who never retaliated against a police officer. Since it was an 80 to 2 ratio of gamblers and cops, the gamblers would provide a certain amount of protection to police officers. They knew a $25 fine would be imposed for gambling and in a sense it was a calculated business expense. But if someone got mouthy, the guy running the house would firmly tell patrons to "sit down and shut up" for he knew major outbursts would only bring the police in to shut the place down permanently.

Gambling games could be very danger-ous however, because hijackers knew wherever there was a game there would also be a lot of money. Robbers would barge into a game, guns drawn and usually rough up the crowd before taking everyone's money. They knew full well the gamblers wouldn't report being robbed because they were breaking the law by gam-bling. The gamblers usually just wrote it off as a business expense.

I learned the lesson of always carrying a little change in my pocket after a raid on a bar in the wee hours of the morning. I had been told gambling was taking place at this location. The bar lights were on well after hours, and I figured right that gambling was in full swing in the back room. From outward appearances, this looked like a small bar. I didn't know there was an add-on room that would hold approximately 200 people.

When I entered the front door, I only saw about 10 people including a bartender. I really felt at this time the only violation I had to deal with was serving alcohol after hours. So when my partner and I entered the building, I locked the door behind us, not wanting these patrons to leave before I gathered names and addresses.

Immediately I rushed to the bar to gather the drinks as evidence. During this commotion I found myself facing a drunken crowd of nearly 200 mad patrons emerging from the back room where a gambling game had indeed been in progress, although neither my partner nor I had detected a crime.

A riot was just about to ensue. Everyone wanted out of the place and I being a lone police officer in the way. I realized I had no radio to call for backup and the only telephone in the joint was coin operated. With not a dime in my pocket, I opened the cash register and took out a dime, using it to call headquarters to send backup units. Lucky for my partner and myself, we weren't far from the station. The owner complained about the police using his dime to make a call for help.

Despite the lack of change in my pocket,

rating reports from the vice squad came back with rave reviews—dedicated, hard working, loyal police officer that worked well with others.

After hearing of my expertise in gambling, the California State Racing Authority at Hollywood Park and Santa Anita offered me a part-time job. The law doesn't allow anyone to be on a racetrack that has been convicted of immoral acts, gambling or prostitution. Walking the racetrack every day, the same people I'd arrested for those infractions were escorted off the property.

One of the things I looked for at the racetrack was touting, and this is still an illegal practice on most tracks. A tout will approach a track patron and state he has inside knowledge of which horse will win the next race. For a mere $10, he'll let that patron in on the winner. If there are nine horses in a race, then the tout is sure to have at least one happy customer.

Before the next race, the tout would find that lucky winner and make him believe he knew the winner of the upcoming race. This time, however, it would cost a $100 for that knowledge. After all, the customer was already a winner. At this point, unless by some chance the horse would win, the patron never sees the tout again. Most touts are working for their own gambling money.

Horse racing enthusiasts are an odd breed that tries to take every advantage of old lady luck. One of their habits is that they will always stand or sit at the same place every time they visit the track. In a crowd of 40,000 people, I could always find the person I wanted to see because I knew he would be in the same place where I spotted him yesterday, proving people are true creatures of habit.

It was during one of these days at the track, my partner and I walked through one of the men's restrooms and discovered a gay male trolling the john, dressed in painter's clothing. My partner and I exited the bathroom and discussed who was going to have the detail of operating this man.

My partner lost and returned to the facility to see if he would be approached with an offer ofa lewd act while I waited outside for my partner's signal.

About this time the horses were coming around the track, and the noise was deafening with patrons screaming. But I never heard my partner's cries for help.

So I returned to the bathroom to find my partner and the suspect rolling in an open wall-to-wall urinal. Wet, smelly and a little shaken, the suspect was arrested and my partner consoled.

I don't remember him ever operating a gay again. From that day forward, he would always say he didn't care if they wanted to fall in love in the john, adding, "I'm not going in there."

After the last race of the day, you find anywhere from 20,000 to 40,000 people heading for the parking lots. A few emerged winners, about 10 percent at best.

We would usually see a large crowd gathered, this signaled a three-card Monty game was underway. One man would get on his knees with three playing cards, two black aces, one red, flopping them from left to right in a hurried manner, saying, "Can you guess where the red ace is?"

There would always be a shield, or partner in this crime, acting as if he were a better. The shield would appear to be winning large amounts of money from the dummy on his knees with the cards. This was the same as the find the pea in the nut game.

The dealer can truly prove that the hands are quicker than the eye. But the shield appearing to win, makes the game look easy, telling passersby, "Come on, get in this game. Get your money back."

It seemed the losers leaving the track were always willing to join the game.

The three-card Monty players would have other partners in the crowd as lookouts for undercover officers. We would try to approach this game while the suspect was on his knees for it was always a foot race when the time for arrest was imminent.

Bookmaking, a low-grade felony, is just another form of gambling and the City of Los Angeles had its share of participants, with estimated betting ranges in millions per day, all on horses and sports. The business is so lucrative the mob can frequently be found running these operations.

Infiltrating bookie operations was a slow process, taking weeks to investigate.

Every bookie has several locations and generally they hire a widow woman to sit and take down numbers. The parlor has a business front but a quick clue to the type of operation will be several people with horse racing forms and pamphlets scattered on the desktops.

Not unlike other gamblers, their unique lingo flowed from the lips of bookies, a telltale sign of their operation. Calls to a bookie would include certain phrases. For example, "Give me number three in the third race, two dollars across the board, at Los Alamedas," translated to the number three horse, in the third race at Los Alamedas to win, place or show.

The tracks can change, it may be Santa Anita or Hollywood Park but the jargon is the same.

A $3 scratch sheet is used, determining races, horse positions, jockeys, and opening odds.

The most a bookie pays is $99 on a $2 bet, where the track pays whatever the real odds are. The odds aren't as good with the bookmaker as they are at the track, but you don't have to get in the car or ride a bus downtown and fight 40,000 people to make a wager. More people place bets on losers than winners so the bookie screws the racetrack and the State of California out of profits.

The bookies used several different methods of recording the numbers until after the race, always having an easy way to destroy these bets if the vice squad arrives at their location.

One bookie wrote bets on grape chewing gum. When we arrived he would put it in his mouth to destroy the evidence. He did this so often he became deathly ill at the sight of grape flavored gum. Officers got wise to this practice and would take out grape chewing gum, offering him a stick when they came to visit. The mere sight of it would make the bookie turn green and throw up. Nine pieces of grape gum per day for a 30-day span would be enough to make most people regurgitate.

Other bookies used flash paper to record bets, pays and owes. They always kept a candle lit nearby. Flash paper, normally used by magicians, is impregnated with gunpowder. When officers would come to visit, merely waving the paper over a lit candle, and poof, the paper disintegrated.

Some bookmakers used a small Formica board could easily fit into a pocket. A water bucket and Ajax would scrub the numbers clean at the end of a day. That was a few years prior to the mass production of dry erase boards but the principle was the same.

One way for officers to screw with a bookie was to seize all his numbers, destroying his livelihood. Many times policemen would leap over the counter of a bookie's office and immediately try to grab the evidence before the bookie could wipe the slate clean.

Arresting the owner, known as the back office, of the operation was a difficult task, akin to trying to nab a drug kingpin. As with drug arrests, usually the small fish, a little pregnant woman sitting behind the counter got arrested, and the bookie in the back office got away.

Destroying the pays and owes could destroy a bookie operation. If the pays and owes records were taken as evidence and the bookie arrested, word went out on the streets immediately. You can bet as soon as he was released from jail, all the customers would swear they bet on long-shot winners. This could usually cost a bookie more than the legal expenses and fines.

A now famous attorney that was involved in the O.J. Simpson case, represented many bookies during the early days of his career. Too busy to find a parking place several blocks away, he parked his Rolls Royce in a drop-off zone in front of the Los Angeles County Courthouse. LAPD officers scrambled to give him a ticket almost on a daily basis.

I credit much of my expertise to a mentor at a high-class gambling parlor. I met up with an older black gentleman who had traveled all over the world and played cards professionally on several continents. The soft-spoken gentleman showed me much of what put me in the category of becoming an expert. The circuit this gentleman traveled in was a higher class of people, like is portrayed in the movies. He never fought the police during arrests, and always graciously paid the fine imposed.

I would listen to his tales for hours while he explained different card games, odds, what a mechanics grip was (the method of dealing from the bottom of the deck). He would teach how to flip the cards and see if the deck was marked by watching the spoke on the wheel turn if it were a Bicycle brand of cards. Each brand of cards would be marked in its own style where a true cheat could read the backs as well as the front side. He was a wealth of information and never seemed to mind teaching me the trade.

In Los Angeles, an officer can only work vice for a two-year period to deter corruption within. The old adage can become true "when you roll in shit long enough, you soon start smelling like it." Superior officers handed down the notice and I would return to patrol the following weekend.

But something happened I am yet to understand today. My first Saturday night off the vice squad, two vice officers went to the black gentleman's door where a gambling game was in progress.

As they entered, like I'd done on many occasions, everyone inside seemed to be frightened and ran around hysterically.

The gambler I'd known to be a friend ran to a back bedroom and stood beside the door. As the new officer entered, a gun battle ensued. The officer and gambler were both wounded.

I never understood why because I was always welcome in the gentleman's place of business. Maybe the man got spooked and thought it was a robber because the place was a good target to find large quantities of money and jewelry, and the grandfatherly gentleman wore fine clothing and drove a shiny Cadillac. It had been only a few weeks prior that hijackers entered his game, robbing all of his clients.

I can remember going to court to testify that I had told the other officers about this gambling location. As I entered the courtroom, I tried to catch this gentleman's eye but he wouldn't look up.

He plead guilty, was sentenced and I never saw him again.

I may never know for certain exactly what happened between the gentleman gambler and the police on that fateful day.

Chapter Seven

Teaching the Trade

Now that my superiors had deemed a change, I received orders to report in uniform to 77th patrol division as a training officer. I picked the midnight to 8 a.m. shift because it was a time when the city came alive.

As a training officer, I worked side by side with rookies fresh out of the academy. The goal was to instill good habits that would keep them free from harm while protecting and serving citizens.

An average of 20 radio calls per shift came for me to answer each watch. At that time of night it seemed the calls were always unusual. Domestic calls were always the most dangerous because at that time of night, most people were at a boiling point by the time the police arrived. There was still time for much investigation, patrolmen never wrote too many tickets or investigated a lot of accidents because there was a traffic division to handle those calls.

As for myself I never wrote very many traffic tickets, not that there weren't any violations of the law. You could always find cars with no taillights, no brake lights, cracked windshields, bad mufflers and cars that smoked a little too much. I just hated to write these people tickets—if they had the money to fix their cars they would, so they sure as hell couldn't afford to pay a ticket. It was my personal preference; I know these things should be fixed. If it were something to keep them from killing themselves or others, then sometimes a ticket was needed.

I received a strange call one hot summer evening. There was unknown trouble at a residence. But when I knocked on the door, nobody answered.

The second call came same as the first—unknown trouble, so I went to the house again. This time my partner and I forced open the door only to find a 700-pound woman lying nude on the bedroom floor. She had gotten up in the middle of the night to go to the bathroom and fallen.

If you've ever tried to pick up a 700-pound naked lady, you'll know there are no handles and the task is damned near impossible.

One small-framed officer around 5 feet 9 inches tall and weighing only 150 pounds, assisted by four other officers, attempted to help the lady back into bed. He was standing behind the woman when she fell backward, pinning him against the bed. It was sweltering hot in there and the officers couldn't get her off their fellow officer.

She was screaming, he was screaming, and both were very embarrassed.

The back injury the officer received was so severe; he later had to retire because of the injuries sustained that night. I always wondered how he explained that injury to his grandchildren.

Not long afterward, a medical emergency summoned us to a residence where a large, elderly woman was lying on her couch in a housecoat, sweating profusely, suffering from an apparent heart attack.

She was asking for mercy so I got on my knees in front of the woman, trying to talk to her and comfort her by saying that an ambulance would be there in a minute. Afraid she was dying, the woman grabbed me and wedged me between her breasts. I could not break free from the woman's clutches. Now I know full well what they mean by a death grip.

Although situations sometimes seem embarrassing, to have an ambulance crew witness such a sight, to that woman, the policeman was life.

Traveling from one radio call to another, utilizing basic first aid techniques became second nature.

A new recruit was with me when we found a woman carry a baby waking the streets around three o'clock in the morning. She wanted to go to her mother's home for safety reasons, after being involved in a vicious family dispute. The woman was put in the back seat with the partner-in-training. The next thing I knew, my partner was screaming for help.

Apparently this woman suffered from epileptic seizures, most probably brought on that evening from fighting with her husband. My partner was trying to keep the baby from getting hurt, the woman from harming herself, as well as keeping himself from harm's way.

Contrary to popular belief, it's not a good idea to stick your finger into the mouth of someone having a seizure. That's a real quick way to get a finger bitten off. The only thing that can be done is to keep the person from harm until the seizure subsides.

Fear does different things to different people.

Another new officer right out of the academy was on duty when a code three call, robbery in progress, came over the radio. He was driving for the first time; I think all recruits remember the first time they drove.

Red lights and sirens blaring, racing down the boulevard at a high rate of speed, the officer ran right through a red light, without slowing down or looking, causing me to nearly run my brake foot through the floorboard and have a panic attack.

So I reached down and turned off the key, bringing the car to a halt as I told him, "we don't do anybody any good if we don't get there and we could kill someone else."

It was always hard to see what the poor people had to endure. I remember taking a burglary report where a young couple came home from work to find their house ransacked and TV stolen. They were in tears, they had just purchased the TV and now they would have no TV to watch, yet the payments continued.

As I left this scene, about three blocks away, I saw a young man in an alley carrying a TV on his shoulders. This TV turned out to be the one stolen from the couple I had just visited. His intention was to sell it for a mere couple of bucks to buy drugs. Now I know that my job was not to punish but to merely arrest offenders, but it's sure hard to keep from being involved in a brutality case when a situation like that arose.

Judging who is the victim and who is the suspect can sometimes be difficult as was the case with the older white gentleman that owned a south end liquor store just outside Gardenia.

The liquor store had been burglarized on

several occasions, each time the same method of operation used by the suspect. A milk crate was used to break out the front window, then the burglar loaded up a gunnysack filled with cigarettes and booze.

The owner told me he was going to sleep in the back room on a cot and wait for the next hit. I advised him to be very careful.

Not a week later the call came out needing an ambulance to respond to a shooting at the same location.

The old man was visibly shaken when I arrived. After disarming him, the gentleman said he was awakened from his cot in the back to find a man filling up a gunnysack. He poked a gun into the side of the suspect and told him to stop.

But the suspect turned on him and tried to pull the gun out of the old man's hand in an attempt to overpower the liquor storeowner. The gun went off and one less burglar was alive.

Considering the shaken condition, I stayed with this gentleman until the detectives arrived, wanting to make sure they understood the situation between the storeowner and the burglar.

In a similar incident, I was called to investigate a shooting at an apartment complex. As I arrived I saw a known gang member lying dead at the foot of the stairs.

At the top of the stairway, a woman and her two young children, all obviously scared to death, met me.

When asked what happened, she said her husband just shot and killed this fellow.

When I went inside her apartment, I found the male suspect sitting on the bed, clutching a small infant, as if using the baby to shield himself from me. I could see the fear in this man's face and it was I he was frightened of. There is no doubt he'd probably never had an occasion to invite the police into his home. And I'm quite certain he believed all the stories about white Gestapo cops that would do him harm.

I assured him I meant him no harm and asked where the gun was. He asked, "You won't shoot me will you?" It was a serious question.

I assured him once again I wasn't there to do him harm but I needed to know where that gun was. Then he said, "Don't hurt my baby, the gun is under the bed."

I took possession of the weapon, handed the mother the baby and placed the suspect under arrest.

I sat down on the bed beside him and told him just what was about to happen. He was under arrest, and I was going to take him down to the 77th Street station where he would be booked for murder. Detectives would talk to him and he would be assigned a public defender, if necessary. I told him I wasn't going to read him his rights because I wasn't going to question him—the detectives would do that later. We were just making idle chit-chat, trying to get through this as easy as possible for both of us.

It was then he recounted how this violent gang member threatened his family at all hours of the day and night for a period stretching into several months. Just because the man feared him, the gang member would always threaten raping the wife, killing the babies and burning the couple's home.

On this night, the gang member arrived, issuing more threats, laughing and hollering. The suspect broke down; he couldn't take any more and shot the gang member as he was walking up the steps.

I knew the story was true and felt sorry he was pushed into such a situation.

The shooter loved to fish, but on the way to jail he told me, "I'll never get to go fishing again."

Being a fisherman myself, I assured him that he would fish again.

It was the only time I ever testified on behalf of a murder suspect. The man had lived in terror for months and the circumstances were unusual. There was an imminent threat because the gang leader had stalked and preyed upon the man.

When the trial was over and the man acquitted, I felt good walking up to him and saying, "I guess you're going fishing today. Well maybe tomorrow, today your wife and children need you with them."

Good judgment is vital. Sometimes an officer has to help people stay out of jail as well as knowing when to put them in jail.

There was always the lighter side as well. One warm night I saw a lone male wearing a long black coat. There had been several bus robberies in the area at the time. In my opinion the long black coat could be worn just to hide a weapon. So I stopped the suspect for questioning.

After a search for weapons revealed none on his person, I asked for identification. At which time he stated he had none. I was in the process of running him for warrants, which was customary, when I saw falling from his pockets, several red capsules resembling a popular drug on the streets at the time, Secenol.

When it came back on the radio there were no outstanding warrants, I advised the suspect he was under arrest and retrieved approximately 25 red capsules from the sidewalk. I booked the suspect for possession of illegal drugs.

During a court appearance, I testified to the above events. At that time, the defendant jumped up and stated angrily, "You couldn't have seen me drop those red pills, you're framing me, you had your back turned."

With that, the judge ruled guilty as charged.

Working patrol, officers get protective of their beat. They become proud to take care of a particular domain and when assigned to it they are sometimes territorial and don't want other officers to work it. But that's hard to do in a big city.

A liquor store near Broadway and Florence Streets had been broken into, the front window busted and the store pilfered. Calling the owner, he advised there were guns underneath the counter. Thinking there were still suspects inside, this posed a great risk to officers.

My partner was deployed to the back while we were waiting for the owner to bring a key. In the meantime, SWAT officers came in and advised they were taking over the scene.

"This is my call and my area, and I will handle it," I told them firmly. "We're trained to do these things without getting hurt. I'll be the searching officer, arresting officer and I will do the paperwork," I explained.

Tempers flared and heated words were exchanged before we finally agreed to search the building together for hidden suspects. Four suspects were arrested; all found holed up in the store.

The sergeant on duty was really mad about my actions.

Although I didn't realize it at the time, my days on patrol were numbered and the territory I'd been staunchly protecting would soon change.

The same sergeant that had been so angry the day previous promoted me to metro squad the following morning.

Chapter Eight

Metro Division

A new kid on the block, I didn't care who my partner said this man was, I demanded David Carradine provide some form of identification.

An opening was available in metro division. Metro had four teams—A team was administrative, B team worked the valley, C team worked the south end and D team was SWAT.

Metro was a 200-man squad that took care of the entire city and worked every facet of law enforcement. You could be assigned anywhere, at any time of day or night. Officers checked in after each shift to see what duties would be performed the next day and what uniform would be worn. Some details would require wearing a uniform, but other times it was deemed a suit and tie, or even hippie attire. Whatever the attire, the job proved to be exciting because it was different every day.

This position was a very sought after job with the Los Angeles police department. It was known to have the very best and most aggressive police officers among the 7,000 officers from which to choose.

Details would include VIP security, stakeouts, patrol, loaned to narcotics, robbery, homicide, or any other division that needed extra assistance.

"Why would you want me," I asked, clearly puzzled the sergeant would give me a second look considering how angry my superior had been just the day before.

"I respect you not wanting to turn over your scene," the sergeant replied. "The way you handled yourself when you got in, I know you're not afraid to do your duty and we have an opening. Let me know in three days."

The move was a difficult decision. The 77th division had become home turf. I was the senior man on patrol and if I took the position I would be going to low man on the totem pole. At metro, I would be trained instead of training others. With an average of 15 to 20 years service at metro, officers rarely left the metro unit for they had a take-home car and most officers lived at least 40 miles from the station. You always worked with a good partner and got the very best assignments so making sergeant and going back to morning watch patrol didn't really have that much appeal.

I accepted the assignment and found myself thrust into the position of new kid on the block. It didn't take me long to realize, I didn't know the players in this game and I didn't have a program.

A major obstacle to overcome was the citywide jurisdiction in which the metro squad worked. I didn't know how to work with middle or upper class white people. In Watts most everyone was Negro or Hispanic. But in the valley, the banker could very well be the bank robber driving a Mercedes, or the doctor's son a dope dealer sporting around town in a Jaguar.

While working crime suppression with my new partners in Hollywood division, a new area for me, I saw a vehicle parked in the middle of the street near Hollywood and Vine. The car was causing other drivers to have to go around it. A lone male was pouring gas from a one-gallon gas can into the vehicle.

I called him to the sidewalk and asked to see some identification. He told me, he didn't have any I.D. with him but his name was David Carradine.

"My name is Bill Myers and I have a driver's license to prove it," I retorted.

Quickly realizing the star, my partner said to me, "Okie this is David Carradine."

"Well he just told me that, but I still need a driver's license," I persisted.

"You know this is the actor from Kung Fu," my partner explained.

I stepped back and ordered, "Don't even look at me like you want to do any Kung Fu shit on me. I need an I.D. and I need this car moved out of the street."

Carradine assured me he knew nothing about martial arts, his work was done in slow motion by a dance routine.

Years later, my cousin, a Kung Fu enthu-
siast, sent me a photograph that appeared in a
magazine of David Carradine, my partner and
myself. I never saw anyone around with a camera that day.

Although I didn't know the turf or the
players too well in Hollywood, the insight
gained working prostitution in Watts paid off
one cold December night. The streets were quiet
as I along with a seasoned officer that had never
worked vice before, were cruising along when I
spotted a streetwalker and said to my partner,
"Let's go visit with her, she might have drugs.
She's definitely working the streets."

A closer inspection revealed the needle
track marks up and down her arms associated
with a full-fledged hype. An arrest could be
made when a suspect was high and there were
fresh scab-colored marks, as was clearly evi-
dent with this prostitute.

"I'm taking you to jail because of the
marks," I told the streetwalker. Knowing she
would get sick if institutionalized and unable to
get the next fix, I added, "Tell me who your
supplier is and I might be able to cut you
loose."

The streetwalker agreed to call her dealer

and ask him to bring a piece of heroin delivered inside a condom for an agreed price of $1,000. She made the call. After a policewoman searched the girl to make sure any drugs she might come up with later was not something she had been carrying all along, we put her on the corner to wait.

But the minute she got out of the dealer's vehicle after the buy, she broke into a run, tossing the evidence to the ground, attempting to flee the scene. She was chased down, her dealer cuffed on the spot. Her little role-playing fighting arrest looked good—she could have won an Oscar award for it.

The dealer was taken to jail but as promised the streetwalker was set free, a decision that probably could have gotten her killed. Being a three-time loser, the dealer was looking at some serious jail time, so the defense kept asking for a postponement to search for the prostitute he'd been with at the time of the arrest. She would testify for him that the police merely put a case on him with no reason at all. He didn't know she had set him up.

I presumed she, like most heroin addicts, was a transient and had long since left the area.

After I testified and as I stepped out of the courtroom and into the hall, I was met by the frightened streetwalker who wanted to know, "What am I gonna do? If I tell that court I snitched him out he'll kill me." She had been found in Civil Brand Institution, the Los Angeles County jail for women, where she had been incarcerated for some time.

All I had time to tell her was "stand on your fifth."

In the hallway, I perspired through my suit while waiting for the girl to complete her testimony and exit the courtroom. When I asked what she'd said, she advised she'd pleaded her fifth amendment.

The suspect was convicted and sentenced.

Thereafter, when I trained officers I reminded them never to make a judgment call that would put someone's life in jeopardy. "Take the case just as it is because you can't shovel shit against a tide," I would warn each trainee.

Throughout my career I can see how violently people can become when trust is betrayed and police are notified a crime has been committed.

While working crime suppression detail in the valley early one summer morning as we turned a corner, my partner and I were alerted to loud screams emitting from a residence.

Inside the house was a man holding a bath towel around his neck, throat split from ear to ear. We threw him into the patrol car and drove the man to emergency room personnel waiting at a nearby hospital; luckily it was just around the corner, two blocks at the most.

When the doctor began to question the man about how this happened, he said his live-in girlfriend did it. The victim said after he'd had a few drinks and consumed some Church's fried chicken, he wanted to make love.

His girlfriend agreed to have sex with him, even though earlier in the evening she'd suspected her boyfriend of cheating on her.

In the heat of passion, the girlfriend straddled him. "The next thing I knew, she cut my throat," the victim recalled. Around 400 stitches were required, 200 inside and 200 outside. He would have bled out in a short time had it not been for us.

We went back to the residence and had to make a forceful takedown of the girlfriend, fighting arrest.

"He's been so shitty and I'm going down," the girl said. "He steals credit cards, they're under the carpet."

Sure enough, beneath the rug we found stolen credit cards, forcing us to take the man in custody.

And although I'd saved the man's life, he hated me worse than the woman who turned him in.

I have observed during my career different ethnic groups possess certain traits during the heat of a domestic dispute.

The Hispanics are more prone to knives and cutting, whites will often pick up a gun or beat a family member, and members of black families will revert to scalding, throwing a pan of hot grease that would mark the victim forever.

Nobody was more shocked by weird self-infliction than an elderly black couple that received a very unexpected visitor.

A young white man had busted into their home, they told a dispatcher, making an outrageous claim that the couple were his mother and father. When I arrived, the grief-stricken black couple pointed me in the direction of a white man lying on their couch.

"I'll prove to you I'm your son," he told the couple. Grabbing a butcher knife he whacked off his own finger.

One thing I was amazed at was the wound didn't bleed. An ambulance crew arrived, placed the finger in ice, took care of the injury and shipped the guy, probably high on

LSD, on to the mental facility.

It would not be the first or the last time that I would run into a mentally deranged person.

Working San Pedro one evening, a car came up alongside the unmarked police vehicle, and the driver began staring at us. When we stopped at a red light, he pulled his car so close to ours that it would have been impossible for my partner to open his door, fearing being trapped inside the vehicle. My partner threw our vehicle into reverse because he didn't want to be trapped inside the car.

As I opened my passenger door, the man began spitting on the front of my patrol car and took off running.

"I don't want to work late tonight," my partner insisted. "Let's go home, he's a nut."

Nearly ready to give up and leave, as I got back into the vehicle, the suspect, run back to the car and spit on it again.

The cat and mouse game continued until the man ran past me while attempting to spit on the car for a third time. Within arms reach, I nabbed the guy by the collar. In a split second, we were asshole over elbows, with the guy growling at me like a dog. I got to my feet and was holding the man's head away from me.

He began to try to bite me, so I promptly
smacked him up side of the head with a baton.
Blood flew. There was no doubt in my mind
that this man was not only going to bite me, but
really sink his teeth into me, not a poodle bite,
but a pit bull bite.

My partner was no help at all, laughing
uncontrollably on the sidelines. He stepped in to
help when the third blow was struck and the
suspect still continued to try to bite my leg,
growling all the while.

The emergency room doctor thought I
had beaten the man unnecessarily. But what if a
citizen had met up with the crazy man; any
ordinary person on the street would have been
hurt badly from all the biting.

One partner I worked with for a very
short time, for some reason wanted to be a
good guy so badly; he failed to exercise common sense on many occasions. It was always,
"Maybe we can help this poor soul." But some
people just don't want help. One late evening I
drove this partner to the station and told the
watch commander we didn't work well together
and he was going to get someone killed.

Up until this period of time, he'd been a
great officer; we had played golf and fished
together on many occasions. It was only a few

nights later several units were called to a male mental case wielding a gun. When we arrived, a man was standing in the middle of a residential neighborhood waving a shotgun around, threatening anyone or anything.

From a position of concealment, as we tried to talk the suspect out of this situation, without warning this officer stepped out and yelled, "Don't shoot," to everyone involved.

It was as if the officer felt someone would fire on this suspect without more provocation. He walked toward the suspect, who was as surprised as anyone else, and said, "I'm not here to harm you, give me the gun."

As the officer reached toward the weapon, the suspect fired point blank into the officer's right hand, causing him to lose his arm just below the elbow. The suspect lost his life in a volley of gunfire.

Sadly, you just can't be nice to everyone on the street at all times.

Metro provided me with my one and only job working in a business office. Several bank robberies occurred in a short period of time, so the LAPD planted officers in the bank on a special stakeout. My partner and I became bank clerks at Security Pacific National Bank's branch at Washington Avenue and Vermont

Boulevard.

Unobtrusively, cops had to blend the special assignment with the task of processing paperwork associated with being a bank clerk. This was all done without the knowledge of any bank employees, including their supervisor. Surprisingly, we performed our tasks well and received compliments from unsuspecting bank employees on a job well done.

We sure as hell didn't act like loan officers because all we had was clerical job and counted a little money.

In a commendation we received the bank president described the undercover officers from Los Angeles as "the finest in the nation" that also turned out to be pretty good bankers as well.

Stakeouts were a frequent occurrence; most were boring hurry up and wait jobs. One such excursion stands out more than the others.

My partner and I were working a liquor store in the valley, watching for an armed robber that had been frequenting the area. Parking undercover cars a long way off for backup, we positioned ourselves inside a beer cooler.

This task would require all the clothes you could put on, with a stocking cap pulled down over our ears and gloves. It may have been cold inside the refrigerated unit, but outside it was within the 90-degree range.

Sitting inside the cold storage unit for eight hours became rather boring until a very attractive blond customer headed toward the cooler—donned in a minimal amount of clothing that included a revealing top.

As she bent over to get a six-pack, my partner was unable to resist. He pulled some of the beer back forcing the pretty girl to bend over, nearly falling out of her dress, as she reached further into the beer cooler.

When her hand reached for the six-pack, he gallantly kissed it. You would have thought he had cut her hand off the way she screamed. The store patrons and people in the street didn't have a clue what had happened.

She ran out of the store. To this day, the woman probably tells her grandchildren the story.

This same partner was responsible for me being shot the one and only time during my career. After all the situations I'd found myself involved in, the shooting happened following a long stakeout and the arrest of a liquor store robber we'd been after for some time.

We decided to celebrate with a drink of Old Crow in my partner's garage when I took him home that evening. A few good laughs, a few more drinks from the bar set up in the middle of the garage floor, we continued telling war stories until wee hours of the morning.

Around 3 a.m. we were still reliving the events of the day, when all of a sudden there was a loud percussion, I mean an eardrum-breaking kaboom. Knowing full well my partner's love of practical jokes, I immediately hollered, "Damn what was that? What the hell did you do?"

He looked as if his heart had failed him, weakly replying, "Nothing. I didn't do any-thing."

By now I was rubbing my left knee be-cause of a sharp pain. Looking down I saw his right pants leg blown wide open from the seams.

Regaining our composure, the story unfolded. He had a three-inch .38 revolver in his right pocket and for reasons unknown to any-one but him, he was cocking and un-cocking it as we spoke—just a nervous reaction. Not even realizing what he was doing, the gun fired in his pocket, the bullet traveled downward, between his sock and foot without hitting meat. Striking the cement floor, the ricochet entered my right knee, stopping without breaking the bone.

My partner's leg was black with powder burns and it had to be painful. We pulled the lead from my knee, cleaned the wound, and made a vow not to mention the episode until we had retired. An accidental shooting was good for two or three days off without pay and in metro, possibly a transfer back to patrol. After all we worked with guns, they were tools and we knew better than to play with them.

We both limped back to work the next day knowing full well we were lucky not to have been injured more seriously.

Chapter Nine

The Longest Day

Fellow SWAT members formulate plans for an upcoming mission.

The time came while working metro that two officers had been promoted from the SWAT team. I volunteered for that duty and was accepted in 1972.

This was an assignment foreign to me although I had spent four years in the Navy; I had never been involved in combat missions, so the operations and maintenance of automatic weapons was not something I was familiar with. Most SWAT officers had served in the Marine Corps and had experienced combat duty training.

In the early years on the SWAT team, each member had to purchase his own equipment, with the exception of the weapons. We would train at Camp Pendleton with the Marine Re-Con division. While we were there we would buy military green fatigues, hats and combat boots. This was still in the experimental stage for law enforcement so the LAPD wasn't going to purchase these items for us. I had to start at entry level; everyone laughed because they had to teach me the basics like blousing my pants.

We had a rigorous workout routine. It was mandatory that we stay in shape for you can't protect anyone if you're trying to get a breath of air after running up two flights of stairs while wearing full combat gear. We did take one hour out of every workday for training at the police academy and had to pass a physical fitness qualification (PFQ) every 60 days.

We also were familiarized with our weapons weekly and spent hours on the firing line where every man became an expert. I was probably the worst marksman of the bunch. We also trained on the fire towers and later on, out of helicopters, the art of repelling. I still can't believe that I went out of a copter on a rope because I'm still, and always have been, afraid of heights. But this just goes to show how much faith I had in my fellow officers, they knew my phobias and could talk me right down. All of our lives depended on each other daily. When I knew we were having a training day that involved repelling I used to stew over it weeks in advance. When my partners came to pick me up I was so nervous, they nearly had to carry me to the car.

There were good and bad times, but we never knew what a day could bring. The 60-man unit was known as the best in the United States, possibly throughout the world. We formed a bond that will never be broken, through it all. At that time I thought we were in the best physical shape a man could possibly be, and I thought we had the best equipment. Visiting with new SWAT team members today, I see quite a change. Most look like bodybuilders, can run for miles and literally leap buildings in a single bound, using weapons today that made our old stockpile look like pea shooters. Now I realize it's a wonder we lived through the many missions we endured.

In the old days our missions were to protect the lives of officers and citizens through our training and armament expertise. When a patrol division requested our assistance there were certain criteria that had to be met: An imminent danger to officers; suspect had to be barricaded; and weapons had to be used in the crime. Very seldom did we assist in search warrants but there were a few occasions. We didn't just roam from division to division taking over situations. Each division had to request our assistance.

My first day with the SWAT team I was called in by my immediate sergeant and watch commander and told I would be working with two officers that had a reputation of being two of LA's finest.

But these officers were known at times to be a little aggressive. It was my assignment to protect them from the citizens and often times themselves. Serving 4-5 years with the SWAT unit, both had reputations as hard workers, but were also notorious for taking risks. I found this would be a full time job.

We worked in five man squads, two squads forming a team. There was always one team of SWAT officers on call 24 hours a day. We drove unmarked vehicles and carried all of our SWAT gear in the trunk. The first team on the scene of a SWAT mission would find a command post nearby the objectives and out of sight. The rest of the team would form up and formulate plans. Literally getting dressed in an alley or parking lot was a common occurrence.

My two new partners and myself worked one car always two on duty while one was on days off. We traded off so every 28 days one officer got nine days off duty. On occasions when all three partners would be on duty, one of us would work with another SWAT unit that might be missing a man because of sickness or vacation. A man didn't even dream of not answering the phone when he was on call because we were paid to be on call those nine days off-duty.

The SWAT team was responsible for providing VIP security, including guarding presidents, heads of state, foreign dignitaries that were visiting the City of Angels. This particular assignment sounds very distinguished but setting on top of a rooftop for hours or guarding a back fire escape can have a lack of luster. Although there were good times when I was right next to these people, but all the assignments were equal in importance for safety reasons.

Crime suppression and stakeouts, assisting the robbery and homicide division with their investigations, and surveillance of known criminals suspected of committing dangerous crimes was done whenever we weren't on SWAT missions.

We had been assisting robbery/homicide with the infamous West Side rapist case where unknown suspects had broken into homes of elderly women who lived alone, raping and murdering them. This assignment called for numerous hours of stakeouts on the rooftops of buildings overlooking the streets below.

These long hours high above the streets could become very uncomfortable and tiresome. Luckily the weather in southern California protected us from harsh elements and there was very little time for humor. If your mind wandered from the duty for an instant, you might possibly miss seeing a suspect that could result in injury or death to a victim far below.

But on one occasion while on top of a 100-unit apartment building most of an evening, looking at a whole city block, observing pedestrians, and reporting to stand-by units on the ground, my partner and I were up for several hours when he announced, "I wish I hadn't drank all that coffee, now I have to take a leak."

Since we were out of the sight of citizens and it was dark, I said, "Don't tell me about it, just go."

A few minutes later I heard a muffled cry from somewhere below, "Hey, my steaks are getting wet."

Then I observed my partner urinating down a four-inch pipe protruding from the roof.

We were in full uniform walking a beat in the area gathering information from people in the neighborhood that might lead us to the West Side rapist when we were met by a young man in his early 20s and a beautiful young girl.

This young man approaches my partner in an attempt to impress his apparent girlfriend by boasting, "I'm a black belt in karate and if you tried to hit me with that stick (pointing to my partner's baton) I would be able to disarm you without getting hurt."

Hearing this my partner said, "Don't worry, I'm not going to hit you."

"Come on hit me with that stick and I'll show you."

My partner replied, "No we don't want to do that."

Now the young man pleaded, insisting on the confrontation, "I promise I won't hurt you, just try and hit me with your stick. I can take it away from you without getting hit."

Once again, my partner advised the young man to take his girlfriend for a walk and leave us alone.

The young man persisted, "All I want to do is show you how to take a stick like that away from somebody. Come on hit me with it. I can take it away without being struck. I promise I won't hurt you."

I think all the time this young man expected my partner to swing the stick at him like a baseball bat but we were always trained to use our stick in a thrusting motion, not a wild swing over the head.

One more time this man pleaded, "Please try to hit me with your stick."

My partner, thinking I'm sure, the guy really did know how to defend himself, obliged the request. Thrusting his baton rapidly striking the now victim in the solo plexus, causing the young man to drop in a heap to the ground, gasping and moaning for breath.

At which time the young lady stated in the direction of her fallen friend, "He told you three times to take a walk but no, you're a big fucking man." She promptly walked off, leaving the man doubled over in the street.

One night we were called about 4 a.m. to help with a search warrant served on gang members in the south end of Los Angeles. Reports were they had been stockpiling guns at their residence.

We had already searched two locations and were

now approaching the last location for the night, as dawn was rapidly approaching.

My partner and I were assigned the gas gun detail, deployed at the rear of a single-family residence, on the west side of University division.

We entered the back yard accompanied by an entry and search team. The entry was going to be gained through the back door. My partner and I took a position overlooking the back of the house and a bedroom window. We were not to use tear gas unless the entry team was fired upon.

As the entry team knocked on the back door stating in a loud voice, "Police officers. We have a search warrant. Open the door," a shot rang out and I observed one of the entry team officers fall. Now it was our time for action.

Thinking one of my fellow officers had been shot, I ordered my partner to fire tear gas. This would normally be a flight rite rocket type projectile, fired from an M-79 grenade launcher type weapon.

But my partner loaded the gas gun with a duster round which has to be protruding into the location intended to be gassed and fired, causing tear gas to spew out into the room.

To my surprise, my partner took off in a dead run toward the bedroom window, breaking the window with the muzzle of the gun and firing the duster round. Then he immediately went down on his knees to reload.

Fearing the suspects from inside would fire on him

from a mere three feet away, I put down cover fire from my location with an AR-15.

Knowing this was not a good tactic, I screamed for my partner to get back. I didn't want to have to shoot over his head. He turned to run in my direction while I covered him.

In the dark of the night and with the excitement of the battle, he ran headfirst into a clothesline where a white sheet had been hung to dry. Running toward me with this sheet over and around him, reminding me of a stunt man that you see in the movies who has set himself on fire.

I'm screaming, "This is no time for your ass to be funny. Get back here now."

As it turned out, the officer at the back door had not been shot, but as he was knocking on the door, a shot rang from inside, just as the officer slipped and fell on some dog shit.

Nobody was injured that day, however our pride was severely bruised.

Those were the kind of things that frequently happened to this particular partner. And it was with this man I spent what seemed like the longest day my career, a day neither one of us will ever forget.

We had worked stakeouts from 10 a.m. until 6 p.m., dead tired from the boredom of watching and waiting on a suspect that had not panned out. We planned on reporting to the station that evening, only to pull our pen (check the schedule) for the next day and report in with the dispatcher on duty.

Arriving at the station, after grabbing a late dinner around 10 p.m., we walked into the office.

We were greeted by our watch commander and should have known something was wrong when he expressed how happy he was to see us, for it seemed sergeants were rarely happy to see us. He then told us everyone else had gone home and he needed two officers for a stakeout in Wilshire Division at midnight.

When we complained and tried to beg off he explained that this was a very critical situation that would most probably end in a shootout. Further explaining the situation, it appeared a young prostitute had wanted to get out of the business but her pimp had other ideas.

It seems this young lady had been a big money maker so her man was not wanting her to leave, giving her an ultimatum—"pay $10,000 in cash and I'll let you go," he told her. She had reported this to Wilshire detectives earlier in the day. She had gone to the bank to meet this extorter with detectives on hand to make an arrest.

This suspect was six foot six, 245 pounds, and meaner than a junkyard dog. He had been a suspect in numerous beatings, assaults and murders on some of the girls that had worked for him in the past. It was said that he carried a picture of a dead girl in a coffin showing this to his stable, letting them know he was responsible for putting her there and the same could happen to them if they got out of line.

At the bank, the pimp met our victim and when the sign was given, detectives moved in and a brawl ensued.

Both detectives were injured and the suspect fled the scene.

Now we were asked to guard the prostitute throughout the night at her apartment. Although tired and weary, we headed off for another eight hours of stakeout.

When we arrived the victim, a beautiful young black woman in her mid-20s, met us at the door. She showed us the layout of her apartment; her boyfriend was also present and was planning on staying the night. I remember she had prepared a full-fledged turkey dinner with all the trimmings for us.

The phone would ring about every 20 minutes and the suspect would be demanding his money. Trying to entice him, she told him, "Come on over. I have your money here. I'm sorry about today. I didn't know those police were there."

He was nervous about the situation but agreed to come to the apartment.

We instructed the victim that if the doorbell rang for her to open the door and immediately turn and walk to the back bedroom out of harms way.

My partner and I sat in the darkened living room for what seemed like an eternity. Around 3 a.m. the doorbell rang causing my adrenaline to soar. With heart beating at a tremendous rate, I stood by one side of the door as my partner faced me with shotgun in hand. The victim opened the door and immediately turned and walked away as instructed.

At this time a female entered the apartment. I kicked the door closed behind her and told her to get on her knees. My partner being very excited, pointed the shotgun at this scared visitor, and stated, "Where is Willy." Further stating, "If he comes to that door and you make a sound alerting him of our presence causing us to get into a shooting, I swear I'll blow your head off first."

"Put down the shotgun," I ordered my partner.

Excited, he said to no one in particular, "I'm telling you, if you get us in a shooting I'll kill your ass."

I again ordered the gun to be put down, this time even more sternly. I'm sure this girl must have been frightened to death with the sight of two officers arguing over her demise.

It seemed that the pimp had sent her in his place to retrieve the money. With the girl handcuffed and seated on the couch we once again waited in the darkness for him to follow. But all that came was a phone call wanting to know where the girl and his money were. At which time the victim told him the young lady had taken the money and left.

No phone calls followed and no suspect arrived that night. At 8 a.m. Wilshire detectives relieved us and took over the stakeout.

At last, we were headed for home with full intentions of dropping my partner off at his home in Wilmington. A bachelor who had a fondness for kids, when we arrived at his house, a little neighbor boy wearing no shirt or shoes wanted his attention badly. Being tired, he walked right to his front door, not giving the child a second glance.

I stepped out of the vehicle and said, "Wait, seems like this little fellow wants to speak with you." At which time my partner bent down and began having a conversation with the little boy.

"Wait Okie," he called to me as I was backing from the driveway. "He says there's something wrong with his mom, she's been hurt and needs help and this little one stayed outside all night."

We turned my partner's television set on and asked the little boy to stay there while we went to check on his mother who lived across the street.

After nobody answered our knock, we entered the back door through the kitchen. The house appeared to be cold, dark and empty.

I went to the right through kitchen and front room then circled back through a hall toward the bedrooms. My partner went to the left, directly to the bedrooms.

As we both reached what appeared to be the master bedroom door, finding it ajar, we identified ourselves as police officers and asked if anyone was home.

With no reply, we entered the bedroom standing at the foot of a queen-sized bed and observed several comforters and blankets but it appeared no one was there. At the head of the bed there were bookshelves and what I first thought was a red wig that had fallen onto the pillow, partially covered with blankets.

My partner went to the head of the bed and took a

hold of the blankets, pulling them up to peer underneath. I could hear a ripping sound as he made this motion. Then I saw the blood drain from his face and it looked as though he wanted to run. I immediately walked toward him and saw the lifeless decapitated body of what appeared to be a young Hispanic lady.

We immediately left the house and called Wilmington division detectives for we were in their jurisdiction.

After what seemed like an eternity detectives arrived on the scene to begin their homicide investigation and took care of the little boy.

Later that same morning, Wilshire detectives decided the pimp wasn't coming back to the see the prostitute after all. Shortly after they left the scene, he arrived. The pimp stabbed the prostitute's boyfriend to death and kidnapped her, driving into the desert near 29 Palms. The California Highway Patrol stopped the suspect vehicle, at which time he shot and killed our victim and was wounded by the CHP in the shootout that erupted.

That was the longest day I ever spent.

Months later I was subpoenaed to court to testify at the preliminary hearing of the pimp. Just prior to my scheduled testimony in court, the district attorney notified me that my presence was no longer needed.

Apparently when health care workers pulled the hospital plugs to transport the suspect to court he died en route.

Chapter Ten

Serial Killers

Working metro and SWAT, you never
could tell where a killer might be apprehended.
Sometimes it would be in the worst neighborhoods, other times a suspect might be found
pillaging among the glitz and glimmer of Hollywood. Or he might leave the state entirely, taking
up the crime spree half way across the country.
You just never knew, but all leads had to be
followed and stakeouts were set up in an attempt to foil a killer.

The Skid Row Slasher was an infamous
case where someone was stalking and killing
winos and derelicts that frequented the Skid
Row section of Los Angeles. Several winos
were killed in this manner with the same ritual
performed after each killing. Candles were
placed around the body and it was thought the
killer went so far as to drink the victim's blood.

In an attempt to catch the Skid Row
Slasher, for months we posed as winos, derelicts and the homeless. We would go to work
at sundown donned in hobo clothing with wine
poured all over ourselves to make the smell and
appearance realistic. We would lay in alleyways,
doorways and old abandoned hotel rooms
waiting for the killer to attack. During this period, it seemed you could never take enough
showers once you got off duty.

There were always covering officers nearby in case you were the lucky one to be attacked; other officers were watching from rooftops above.

Several arrests were made for robbery, petty larceny, for the transients and homeless seemed to be popular victims. They were always stealing from or hurting each other. And if life wasn't bad enough it seemed that other people would travel into this part of town to take advantage of them. It was something I've never understood.

The Skid Row Slasher was arrested months later, far removed from the gutters and alleys in downtown Los Angeles; in the high rent district of Hollywood Hills. He was apprehended as a burglary suspect at the home of one of the rich and famous. He later copped out during mental evaluations to being the Skid Row Slasher and was convicted in the case.

Hours of stakeouts were also worked on the infamous Hillside Strangler case. The Hillside Strangler's method of operation was to pick up prostitutes, strangle them and dump the bodies on hillsides alongside freeway off-ramps.

We worked stakeouts for months, hoping to run into the perpetrator or see him. Not a suspect or clue was found.

A fishing buddy of mine whose wife was a known psychic, commonly called the Scorpio Lady by her friends, telephoned and advised me to go to a certain corner and our suspect worked or lived there.

I really never took any stock in what the Scorpio Lady had to say about the killer. I did take the information to the detective in charge and told him about the Scorpio Lady's message. At the time, both of us felt it was nothing to look into and to my knowledge it never was investigated more than just a drive-by. We really didn't know what to look for, nothing just jumped out at us at the time.

About a year after the case was solved and an arrest had been made in Washington State, I went by the place and found the Hillside Strangler had worked at a upholstery shop at the exact location where the Scorpio Lady said he would be.

I guess if I had it to do over again I would have followed up more on that lead, regardless of how silly it sounded at the time. In my line of business stranger things have been known to happen.

Chapter Eleven

Very
Important
People

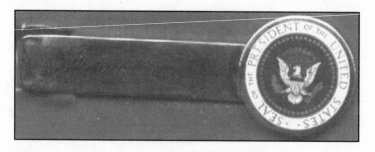

This tie tack was given to me by President Gerald Ford.

Out in the Valley with the rich and elite, it was a place where anything goes and protecting very important people during special events was a task that might find me escorting foreign dignitaries across the city, being a body guard for movies stars and other famous people who receive threats against themselves and their families.

This might sometimes find me living with these families for weeks at a time. These details were always very exciting and the people always treated me as if I were a family member. We went out to dinner, theaters, where this Okie would find himself sampling some of the finest cuisine such as escarole, caviar, sushi and a lots of things my mama never fixed for Sunday dinner.

Former president Gerald Ford was one of the presidents I was assigned VIP security over. I have always been proud to show off my presidential tie tack that he gave me personally.

I had stood my post at the doorway of his room in the Bona Venture Hotel all night when the president emerged early the next morning. He asked if I'd stayed there all night.

"Yes sir, Mr. President," I replied.

He replied, "I'd like to give this to you as a token for your service and I'd like to say thanks for a job well done."

With that, Gerald Ford handed me a little blue box laden with a gold presidential tie tack with his signature embossed onto it. Now we don't accept gifts for doing our job, but you also don't turn down the president of the United States, either.

When the president was coming to town, the Secret Service arrived weeks in advance, for it was their sole responsibility to organize the safest route for the president. They arranged caravan routes, alternate routes for all destinations on the agenda, coordinating these with the local SWAT team since they were the ones that knew the city best.

Some other dignitaries that come to mind that we worked VIP security with was Queen Elizabeth II and her entourage.

For some reason her appearance amazed me. I always felt she dressed rather plainly, wearing a tiny hat, like a little old lady on her way to church. I guess I always imagined her to be smothered in rubies and diamonds and jewelry but this was far from reality. That was just a little Okie in my blood.

Most of my glimpses of her came while I was perched atop a building watching from above, for I was not directly assigned to the

Queen.

A humorous account of the Her Magesty's visit occurred shortly after the plane came to rest on the tarmac. As the Queen was disembarking, a stiff wind suddenly blew her full skirt above her waist.

As she quickly straightened out the garment, my partner grinned and said, "Just how many people do you think have seen the Queen's undies? This has got to be a great job."

We always took VIP security seriously because during a few short years the nation lost Bobby Kennedy in Los Angeles, President John F. Kennedy was assassinated in Dallas and Martin Luther King. The times made this assignment a very serious and real threat.

Chapter Twelve

Patty Hearst & the SLA

UNITED STATES DEPARTMENT OF JUSTICE

FEDERAL BUREAU OF INVESTIGATION

WASHINGTON, D.C. 20535

Keep for Carlos

April 19, 1974

RE: DONALD DAVID DE FREEZE   PATRICIA MICHELLE SOLTYSIK   PATRICIA CAMPBELL HEARST
NANCY LING PERRY   CAMILLA CHRISTINE HALL   MATERIAL WITNESS

TO WHOM IT MAY CONCERN:

     The FBI is conducting an investigation to determine the whereabouts of these individuals whose descriptions and photographs appear below. Federal warrants charging robbery of a San Francisco bank on April 15, 1974, have been issued at San Francisco, California, for Camilla Hall, Donald DeFreeze, Nancy Perry, and Patricia Soltysik. A material witness warrant in this robbery has been issued for Patricia Hearst, who was abducted from her Berkeley, California, residence on February 4, 1974, by a group which has identified itself as the Symbionese Liberation Army (SLA). The participants in the bank robbery also claim to be members of the SLA.

DONALD DAVID DE FREEZE
N/M, DOB 11/16/43, 5'9" to 5'11",
150-160, blk hair, br eyes

PATRICIA MICHELLE SOLTYSIK
W/F, DOB 5/17/50, 5'3" to 5'4",
115, dk br hair, br eyes

PATRICIA CAMPBELL HEARST
W/F, DOB 2/20/54, 5'3", 110,
lt br hair, br eyes

MATERIAL WITNESS

NANCY LING PERRY
W/F, DOB 9/19/47, 5', 95-105, red
br hair, haz eyes

CAMILLA CHRISTINE HALL
W/F, DOB 3/24/45, 5'6", 125,
blonde hair, blue eyes

     If you have any information concerning these individuals, please notify your local FBI office, a telephone listing for which can be found on the first page of your directory. In view of the crimes for which these individuals are being sought, they should be considered armed and extremely dangerous, and no action should be taken which would endanger anyone's safety.

Very truly yours,

Clarence M. Kelley

Clarence M. Kelley
Director

*The FBI wanted poster for SLA members Donald
DeFreeze, Patricia Solttoe, Nancy Perry, Danielle Hall,
and Patricia Campbell Hearst.*

EMILY MONTAGUE HARRIS, nee
Schwartz, 2/11/47, Maryland,
5'3", 108 lbs, blond, blue,
wears glasses Cal DL N2536994

WILLIAM TAYLOR HARRIS, MALE,
CAUCASIAN, 1/22/45, 5'7",
145 lbs, Hazel eyes, Brown Hair,
Calif. Drivers Lic. S 0414078

THERO LAVON WHEELER; ESCAPED
PRISONER AFTER CONVICTION
FOR BATTERY ON POLICE OFF'R
MALE, NEGRO, 1/28/45, Texas,
6'1", 165 lbs, black hair,
brown eyes, dark complexion

PATRICIA CAMPBELL HEARST 2/20/54
5'3", 110 lbs, lite brown medium l
ong hair, brown eyes, fair complexion, mole right side of chin,
scar near right ankle

*During the year-long search for SLA members, police
departments across the nation received these photos of
Emily Harris, Bill Harris, Therro Wheeler, and Patricia
Campbell Hearst.*

One of the most remarkable cases was the Symbionese Liberation Army (SLA), spawned in Berkley, California in early 1970s.

A violent revolutionary group, the SLA declared war against the United States. One of the first violent acts was the murder of Oakland School Superintendent Marcus Foster in 1973. Foster was an advocate of the Black Panther doctrine. One of Foster's crimes, according to the SLA was to issue identification cards for school students.

Another calling card publicized by the group, was the cyanide-laced bullets. The theory behind this would be if you were shot but not fatally wounded the cyanide would poison victims just the same. I don't really believe cyanide was found in any of their weapons but the threat served to panic the public.

On February 4, 1974, newspaper heiress Patricia "Patty" Hearst, granddaughter of multi-millionaire William Randolf Hearst was kidnapped and held for ransom by members of the SLA.

The group sent out many communiqués denouncing numerous government plans and projects. They stated their combat elements had served an arrest warrant on Patty and anyone who came to her aid would be killed. This communiqué was signed "SLA death to the fascist insect that prays on the life of the people."

One such demand was sent to Mr. Hearst ordering him to distribute massive amounts of free food in the San Francisco area, in exchange for the release of his granddaughter. The truck-loads of food started a riot among people clamoring for the goods, but it did not bring the release of Patty.

Nor would any other tactic for nearly two years until on September 18, 1975 when Patty Hearst was captured while jogging in San Francisco with her captors that had since become comrades and co-conspirators.

The SLA leader, Donald DeFreeze called himself SinQ. Meeting his contacts while serving stints of jail time, SinQ and his cohorts robbed banks and amassed an arsenal of weapons.

While Patty was held captive, Sin Q and his followers locked her in a dark closet for weeks and violated this young lady's ever being, constantly causing her to live in fear for her life.

But controversy looms today over her role in the SLA after she joined the group and was photographed during a bank heist. Some people believe Patty was most likely a victim of

when the mind goes to the side of the captor
when life hangs in the balance and the captors
hold the thread.

One other time during my career I witnessed the effects of Stockholm syndrome on a
police officer being held captive by a thug.
When officers outside spoke by phone with the
cop being held against his will, they told him to
try to get the suspect to open a window. The
imprisoned officer turned to his captor and said,
"Don't walk in front of that window."

The Stockholm Syndrome was first
recognized in Stockholm, Sweden when a bank
was robbed and its personnel locked in a vault.
For days they lived in fear in the heat a standoff
between the bank robbers and police. After the
ordeal was over these once victims solicited
money for the defense of the suspects. Some
female victims actually divorced their husbands
and married the imprisoned suspects.

The entire country searched for the SLA
and Patty Hearst. Their famous logo of a seven-
headed cobra and wanted posters appeared in
every newspaper and televised newscasts
across the nation.

At one time Patty sent a letter saying she
was no longer a kidnap victim but rather a full-
fledged member of the SLA and her new name

fledged member of the SLA and her new name was Tanya. She also posed in front of a seven-headed cobra carrying an automatic rifle.

A bank camera later photographed her during a robbery where she was armed with this same type of weapon.

In the spring of 1974 Patty Hearst and members of the SLA were spotted many times in and around the Los Angeles area. SWAT units were called nearly every day with a report of another sighting. We worked each of these sightings as if it were the real thing only to return back to the station empty-handed.

Around 5 a.m. on the morning of May 16, 1974, SWAT units were called to 79th and Hoover Streets in south central Los Angeles. Being one of the first units at the scene, my fellow officers and I were met by approximately 20 FBI agents who told us Patty Hearst, and Bill and Emily Harris were in a house at this location and they wanted to take it immediately, before the sun came up, which is usually a good plan.

We told them we would not take this location until our entire team arrived. Being impatient and unpractical, the FBI alone stormed the house in question, running across the front lawn and kicking in the door of house, located in a middle-class neighborhood just a few blocks from the 77th precinct. The FBI found nobody inside, but literature and debris were strewn about the house, proof that one faction of the SLA, Bill and Emily Harris and Patty Hearst, had in fact been at that location. Had the FBI used that tactic when the SLA was indeed inside, it would have become one of the greatest losses of life the FBI would have ever endured.

One of the agents was overheard saying, "I don't know how they got out. We only left for a short time to get a cup of coffee and donuts."

Later that same day, several SLA members were spotted in a sporting goods store in Englewood, California, located on the outskirts of Los Angeles to the southwest.

A security officer caught members of the group shoplifting Army fatigues and survival equipment. While resisting arrest and fighting their way to the door, Patty was spotted in the van waiting outside the store.

Emily Harris broke free from guards while Patty sprayed the store with machine gun fire. All SLA members eluded authorities.

Now we fully realized the SLA was indeed in southern California. They found evidence the group had been holding maneuvers in the mountains near Los Angeles.

During the morning hours of May 17, SWAT officers on crime suppression detail in Newton Division located the van used in the shoplifting turned robbery and shooting the night before. The van was parked in the drive-way of an abandoned house near 54th Street and Compton Boulevard; it looked as if the noose was getting tighter on the neck of the SLA and the seven-headed cobra.

A stakeout was initiated.

Scheduled for p.m. watch at Newton Division, my two partners and I heard chatter on the police radio about a van that had been spot-ted while en route for our assignment. Several words indicated maybe this would be the night to capture Patty Hearst. We hoped this wouldn't end up being just another drill.

Once at Newton Station a tense roll call was held. Immediately following federal agents were telling the lieutenant in charge of SWAT, a leader for 30 years, that they weren't going to allow the LAPD to take the house in question because the suspects were federal fugitives.

"I don't care how federal the fugitives are, they're in the City of Los Angeles and we're taking them now," roared the lieutenant. "You guys just stay the hell out of the way, we're talking my city now."

There were actually three houses under surveillance and a command post set up at a school on Compton Boulevard. While we were making plans for taking down the first house a woman visited the command post advising officers she had seen several ladies donned in bandoleers at her daughter's home and was afraid for her daughter's safety.

The SWAT team made immediate plans to take that house located two blocks north of the command post and two blocks west of Compton on 54th Street. The immediate block was evacuated to keep citizens from harms way.

I remember as four other officers and myself entered an alley just south of the house in question, I was met by an elderly gentleman who said, "Now you boys be careful." I didn't pay him much heed at the time and we entered a small house to the rear of the suspect SLA hideout, approximately six feet away.

Five other officers were in front of the house. High ground officers were across the street in an apartment building and another sniper placed on top of a garage to watch our backs.

It took several officers to block off the area and members of the press had begun to trickle in on the scene. One female journalist, representing a local television station, had to be physically dragged off the front porch of the house. She insisted on staying so she could interview members of the SLA.

No one ever dreamed of what was about to happen. I had been in on numerous raids at similar locations and usually if gunfire erupted there were two or three shots for show and then the suspect would surrender in front of the press.

Now the command was made from a bull horn blaring from the front, "You in the house, you're surrounded. Exit the house now through the front door."

From my position in the back of the house I could hear furniture being moved for a barricade and I saw an icebox shifted across the back door.

Yet there was no response from the SLA. After two more demands to come out over the bullhorn produced no response, the order was given to fire tear gas from the front.

At that time we used flight rights, a small rocket-type projectile. At the firing of the first flight right, the house lit up like a Christmas tree with firing of fully automatic weapons firing so fast they whistled. We could see all the window shades being blown out in our direction by oncoming bullets.

At this time our lieutenant stated over the radio, "Pour the peter to them boys."

The biggest gun battle in the history of the United States began.

Before the first flight right was fired I remember lifting up the window shade and peering at the suspect house. And as the order to fire tear gas was heard over my radio the officers with me and myself prepared to put on our gas masks.

As that first flight right was fired, my partner, located to my immediate right, bent down to pull up his gas mask and a heavy round struck the wall behind him, right where his head had been. There is no doubt that someone within that house had him sighted in. That round would have been right between the eyes.

Now we were fully involved. I heard him holler, "Okie."

As I turned to look in his direction he was pointing at the bullet hole behind him. I don't think he ever had any fear as they tossed out small pipe bombs loud enough and close enough to cause permanent ear damage.

All I could say was, "Get your ass down."

One of the most frightening weapons fired in our direction was a Browning automatic rifle (BAR) that shoots large rounds. This had been a big game hunting rifle, now converted to a fully automatic weapon. While most of their weapons whistled, the BAR had a definite slow roar, boom, boom, boom, every time it was fired, with the rounds flying over our head and striking the wall behind us. This weapon would be fired and I could see holes appear in front of me, with daylight seeping through the holes. After a short time, the studs were shot out of the wall behind me, the roof nearly caved in around us.

Each SWAT member carried 200 rounds of ammo and I had always thought it was silly to carry that much ammo around in a city like Los Angeles. I scoffed at the idea so many times but this particular day I was grateful. For less than 20 minutes into the fight I was down to one 20-round magazine for my AR-15 and six rounds in my .38 revolver. We were all beginning to get conservative, starting to shoot more slowly because it appeared that we were out gunned and was going to be here for a while.

Finally officers arrived with more ammo but couldn't get to our location due to the heavy gunfire. They ended up throwing boxes of ammo about 50 feet through the windows of our house, bouncing off the walls and sometimes us. We would crawl over and retrieve the ammo and coordinated our fire where some would be firing while others reloaded.

The residue from the gunpowder corroded the ejector slide on my AR-15 causing it to malfunction and become a single-shot weapon. My partners who were firing shotguns had the plastic casings melt inside the chamber, causing their guns to become inoperable.

My greatest fear was that all the SLA members would come out the back door at the same time and rush us, catching us with empty weapons.

Darkness was falling rapidly.

Apparently a flight right struck a Moltov cocktail in side the SLA house and a fire ensued. It wasn't long before their house was totally engulfed in flames.

The heat was intense, tear gas and smoke hung heavy in the air. On several occasions, I had to pull at the bottom of my gas mask to let the sweat escape.

The officer on my left was using a side door to fire from and observe the house. All of a sudden he came under heavy fire. Each time he would try to peer out that door the wood around it would disintegrate. Then he saw one crawl out of a small hole located between the floor of the SLA house and the ground. The hole, designed to inspect plumbing, was approximately 24 inches by 24 inches.

Now we realized the SLA had chopped a hole in the floor and moved underneath the house. One SLA member was coming directly toward us with a handgun in each hand, firing as she came. At the time I didn't realize the shooter was a female; she was dressed in military green, wearing combat boots and a gas mask.

Someone had placed a metal ammo can in the crawl hole for protection and was firing from within, putting down cover fire for the one coming toward us. Fire was returned and this SLA member lay lifeless.

We ceased fire and once again bull-horned, "Your house is on fire. Throw your weapons down and come out. You will not be harmed."

That request was only returned with more gunfire.

The house finally caved in and it was apparent that no survivors would be found inside. However, we couldn't allow firefighters on the scene because of all the gunfire. Even after the SLA quit firing weapons, the thousands of rounds they had stock piled continued to explode for what seemed like hours.

Famed forensic expert Dr. Thomas Noguchi, commonly known today as "the coroner to the stars" was the medical examiner who determined all the victims died underneath the crawl space at the back of the house. Sin Q probably committed suicide, putting a single bullet to his temple.

The SLA swore they would kill 10 officers for ever member they lost that day.

A week after the SLA shooting a helicopter maneuver took a down draft in Fish Canyon, bursting into flames. The commander perished and several crew members badly burnt. At first it was thought to be the works of the SLA.

When it was all said and done, the backbone of the SLA had been broken. Six charred bodies were recovered but Patty Hearst was not one of them.

Fearing Lupe might have seen news accounts of the shooting, just as soon as I got back to the station, I phoned home to let her know I was okay.

"What shooting," came the sleepy response from my spouse.

One of the biggest news events of the century had just occurred and Lupe missed the entire episode.

"Just go back to bed, I'll see you when I get home," I told my wife.

It would be nearly two years, several bank robberies and more deaths, before Patty Hearst and the remaining members of the SLA were captured, ending a war waged against our nation and its citizens.

On September 18, 1975, brought to trial for her part in the Higernia bank robbery, Patty Hearst was convicted and sentenced to serve seven years. In an action by President Jimmy Carter that outraged many in law enforcement and the general public, later commuted the sentence to 23 months.

Other SLA members planted bombs under police vehicles in Los Angeles. On August 22, 1975, all investigations lead to SLA member Kathleen Ann Soliah, reported to have planted the bombs. It took 25 years but in June of 1999, the FBI arrested her under the alias Sarah Jane Olson near her home in St. Paul, Minnesota.

Tips received from viewers after a segment about Soliah was featured on *America's Most Wanted* television show in May of 1999. A $20,000 reward was offered for information leading to her arrest.

After hiding for years, Olson was remembered by acquaintances as a model citizen, a soccer mom married to a doctor. Neighbors were shocked to learn of the arrest

In a federal warrant, authorities claim in 1984 Soliah's husband was aware his wife was a fugitive. It remains unclear she whether or not she was married to her current husband. That same year, she made contact with authorities but negotiations came to a standstill when Soliah wanted complete immunity.

She is currently awaiting trial in Los Angeles for the attempted murder of police officers.

At least one SLA member, James Kilgore, is still at large.

For our efforts on the day of the SLA shootout, a first occurred in the history of the LAPD. My SWAT team earned the first ever Police Commissioners Unit Citation for our acts of heroism.

On July 19, 1974, I received the highest classification of commendation for my part in the SLA shooting that occurred on May 17, 1974 at 1600 hours. It reads as follows:

"On May 17, 1974, Police Officer III, W. D. Myers, serial number 14160, metropolitan division, was assigned as a member of Special

Weapons and Tactics to a task force searching
for members of the Symbionese Liberation
Army. The SLA were believed to be hiding in
the area of 54th and Compton Avenue.

Officer Myers, a member of SWAT Team
2, had been thoroughly briefed by his team
leader, Sergeant McCarthy. He was aware of
recent developments in the SLA case and was
familiar with the history of the organization.
Officer Myers was well aware of both the seri-
ousness and potential danger of the task assigned him.

As the SWAT teams moved into the area
of 54th Street and Compton Avenue, intelligence
was developed which focused the attention of
the task force on 1466 E. 54th Street. A decision
was made to check this location first.

Officer Myers was directed to a position
inside the residence directly behind 1466 E. 54th
Street. A distance of approximately six feet
separated the two buildings. From Officer
Myers' position, he could look through a window and observe part of the SLA dwelling.

As tear gas was fired into the front of the
suspected residence, a tremendous barrage of
automatic weapons fire erupted from the rear
raking the building occupied by Myers and
other officers. Pieces of wood and plaster flew

around the room as numerous rounds struck just above Officer Myers' head.

Officer Myers, upon being ordered by his team leader, took the two northwest windows of the SLA location under fire. It was necessary for Officer Myers to disregard his personal safety and expose himself to hostile fire to do so. He did not hesitate but continued to perform his duty during the entire two-hour period. He continued the same tactic even after a malfunction of his weapon had reduced it to single-shot capability.

Officer Myers is to be commended for the manner in which he accomplished his duties. He displayed tremendous personal courage in fulfilling his mission. Thousands of rounds of ammunition were fired in and around Officer Myers, yet, he remained resolute and undaunted. The volume and intensity with which this battle was waged is unparalleled in the history of domestic law enforcement.

Officer Myers materially contributed to the success of the operation. His performance under conditions of tremendous pressure was the epitome of valor. It was unquestionably a performance dictated by the finest traditions of the Los Angeles Police Department."

I never considered it heroic. Heroism is

when someone knowingly goes into a situation to save one. I didn't have a choice. I was doing a job.

Something I thought about for years afterward is the elderly black gentleman I saw while walking down the alley as we were getting ready to position ourselves inside the house prior to the SLA shootout.

When he told me to be careful he knew what was about to take place, as I'm sure all of the people in the neighborhood also knew something was about to go down. It would have been impossible to move all that armament into a location without being noticed. I'm also sure nobody knew just how big a battle was going to ensue.

In his own way, he was breaking the street code of silence and was trying to warn me. To this day when someone tells me to be careful, I think of that black gentleman. It was an act of kindness on his part.

Members of the LAPD SWAT unit in action as they enter a house during one of their missions.

Chapter Thirteen

Justice for Victims of the SLA

Maybe, just maybe, a big mistake has been made in the investigation of the execution-style murder of a young police officer that I once had the privilege of working beside while on p.m. watch in 77th division (Watts).

During the late 1960s and early 1970s, officer Michael Lee Edwards was a fine young officer who enjoyed his job working 77th patrol and serving the people of south Los Angeles. I can't remember seeing him without a smile on his face coupled with a happy-go-lucky attitude. All the officers that worked alongside him knew full well that he could be trusted in all situations.

I lost track of Mike (as I knew him), when I left 77th division and transferred to metro division. I would see him in court or maybe working the streets when metro was assigned to work crime suppression detail for 77th division. It would be just a passing in the night, maybe backing him up on a radio call or traffic stop, or him backing me up. A brief moment to say, "How's it going," or "keep your powder dry and be safe." I wish now I would have taken the time to get to know Mike even better.

Mike was last seen alive at the police academy on May 10, 1974 at approximately 10:30 p.m. He was off-duty, having a drink with other officers who would often meet at the

Academy Lounge, a club that served dinner and drinks. There was a small dance floor and sometimes a live band performed.

This was a well-known watering hole for a lot of officers. After the watch, and sometimes on their days off, police officers most always relaxed and socialized with other officers, telling war stories only other officers would believe or understand. It was a place where officers felt at ease. There was hardly anyone at the academy but officers, their families or good friends. Sometimes officers from other agencies or someone from the district attorney's office—a place where an officer might let down his guard more than any place else. After all, this was our police academy. Oh yes, and sometimes the place would also fill up with a lot of young ladies that also worked for the police department who enjoyed the company of officers they worked beside and dispatched during the work hours. After all, someone had to use the dance floor.

Mike left the police academy in his personal car and headed to his Long Beach home, located just south of 77th division. In the course of the normal route to Mike's house, one would most likely drive down the Harbor freeway that would take you right through the middle of 77th division, within three blocks of the station house. You would then take the 405 freeway to Long Beach. This trip would normally take approximately 30 minutes at that time of night, for traffic would be light.

Mike was divorcee and engaged to be married, and when he didn't show up on time to his fiancée's home, nobody would worry, for that was the norm for officers. You never knew when you would be working overtime, more often than not extended hours were expected.

It was early the next morning, on May 11, 1974, at 9 a.m., the beaten and stripped body of Officer Edwards was discovered in a fire-damaged one-story vacant triplex in the 100 block of west 89th Street in Los Angeles. He had been handcuffed, shorts placed over his head and shot to death, execution style.

Metro division was notified and every available man was sent to 77th division. We turned the division upside down. Everyone on the street was stopped and questioned. Anyone who could have seen or heard anything was questioned. Even the people on the streets who sometimes felt they had a reason to hate the police appeared shocked at such a brutal crime.

On that same night, a call came in from a citizen stating that a car like the one Officer

Edwards was driving was parked in the 1000 block of 186th Street in Los Angeles. I was one of the officers to arrive at the location and recovered Officer Edwards' car around 11:30 p.m. It was a small maroon vehicle that had a lot of dust and dirt on it, the car of a young workingman. I remember it still had a fishing pole and fish basket in the backseat.

This car was parked at the curb of a single-family residential area near Ascot Park racetrack. The neighborhood was made up of mostly middle-aged white people.

We canvassed the area, going to every door, but could not find anyone who saw who parked the car or anyone around it. It was like the car suddenly appeared at that location. But then, this neighborhood went to bed after the 10 o'clock news every night.

This crime has never been solved. There have been a lot of times during the past 25 years that I have thought of Mike and wish someone would come forward with a lead that could have been followed up on and the people who did this could be held to answer for their crime.

I have to admit that all this time detectives and myself as well, have been looking toward Watts for the answer. I always thought that this was the work of the Black Panthers, another

gang in the area or one of their wannabes. I
always looked, and now I feel everyone viewed
the situation the same; someone in the hood
committed this crime. Now I know that may
even sound racist but it's really not—that's just
where we worked.

It was while I was working on this book
that my opinion has been changed. I now believe the answer has come to me. Sometimes
you can't see the forest for the trees and in May
of 1974, so much happened so fast.

But it was on the 16th of May in that same
year, just six days after the killing of Officer
Edwards that Patty Hearst and the SLA were
known to have been in south Los Angeles.

Remember, they were at 79th and Hoover
that morning, only 10 short blocks from where
Officer Edwards' body was found. They had
committed murders before this, so what did
they have to lose?

At one point in time, Patty herself wanted
to send a communiqué stating that she could be
picked up at a given location and when police
arrived they would be ambushed. This plan was
never carried out, however. After all, in their
mind the SLA was at war with the police. Kid-
napping and murder was part of their game.

Now I truly believe that they went to the

academy where they wouldn't look out of place.
The SLA girls were all easy to look at; one had
even been a topless dancer up north. It is quite
possible that they lured Officer Edwards to his
car, where they ambushed him nearby. For
ambush was also their style.

It would have taken more than one person
to commit this crime. Someone had to drive the
Edwards car, others had to drive Officer
Edwards while keeping him down and it's a
known fact the SLA had a van at their disposal.

It would have been almost impossible for
a black gang member or any black male to get
that close to Mike without being noticed by
someone around the scene. No white officer
would dare go down to the area where his body
was found, particularly alone at night after work.
I felt so strongly about this that I called robbery
homicide division and told this story with my
theory of possibly what might have happened.

Officers on the job today weren't even
out of high school at the time of this killing. I
was glad to know however that a detective is
still assigned to this case full time. He thought
that all the weapons taken from the burned out
SLA house had been tested with no match. I
reminded him that may be the case but they
didn't have all the SLA weapons used at the

time. Patty Hearst, Bill and Emily Harris, and Kathleen Ann Soliah still had a stockpile of weapons and used them at will, not only robbing banks but also committing other murders.

It wasn't long after this that evidence points to SLA members and Soliah placing bombs under the cars of Los Angeles police officers in an attempt to murder them.

I would hope before presidents of our great country could be so freely willing to pardon people because of their rich background that they would make sure they are not perpetrators of terrible crimes upon the citizens of the United States and their police officers.

These members now after 25 years like to go around posing as model citizens. I would hope that this crime will soon be solved and I further hope that this weighs very heavy on Patty's, as well as the other SLA members hearts.

I don't know exactly who was involved but by remaining silent, they are just as guilty as the one that pulled the trigger.

Chapter Fourteen

Forever Blue

Retired Chief Darryl Gates and I pose for a photo at a SWAT dinner in 1997. Chief Gates was not only a boss, but has always been a hero of mine.

Chief Bernard Parks and I also visited during the 1997 SWAT dinner. The city finally got its act together and promoted Parks from within the department.

To put an end of this story is the most difficult of all because for me it will never end.

After the SLA shooting, things became a lot better for the SWAT team. We did a lot more training because when we were really tested we got the job done, but also knew we were very lucky this time around and extensive training was crucial.

We trained every month at Camp Pendleton and taught officers survival at Universal Studios every weekend. We trained officers from every division within the LAPD, officers in other departments across the United States, as well as the secret service and FBI. We were about as close to experts in SWAT tactics and urban guerilla warfare as there was at the time.

Universal Studios was the perfect place for this training. The movie sets were just like streets in our cities and we had the use of all their props.

Aside from all the training, we still performed our duties, stakeouts, VIP security and crime suppression details. We were more in demand now than ever. Now the department was even willing to accept the role of the SWAT team concept. This meant better equipment was being purchased for us but one never knows when they go to work whether it will be their last day or night on the streets.

Two nights in a row I had driven in wild pursuits of stolen vehicles, on both occasions both suspects were arrested without injury to themselves, innocent bystanders or police officers. It seemed I was on a roll—everywhere I looked there was a crime. Or maybe I was just getting better at what I was doing.

My last night on the street began like any other; in fact it was a rather boring detail we were working. There was a rock concert at the coliseum in University division. We were to work the crowd and make sure it didn't get out of hand. This was one of my least favorite assignments. We had worked these concerts on many occasions.

The coliseum would fill up with thousands of young people, music blaring so loud you couldn't hear anything over it. The louder, the better the young people liked it.

It would take no time at all for the place to fill with smoke, some drifting from the stage—it seemed all bands like to use smoke for effect. Some smoke came from cigarettes, and then you could always smell the hint of marijuana smoke lingering in the background.

Beer and drinks flowed freely, you could always bet before the night was over tempers flared and fights would break out. People would be up in the isles dancing to the sounds before long, pushing for better position to see the band or more room to dance. Or a pass would be made at someone's best girl for the night. Some folks didn't need a reason to fight. It was just part of the show, what they came for.

As the fights broke out, we would break them up and take the combatants to a command post to cool off. If that were impossible, they would get a trip downtown, mostly for drunk or disorderly conduct, sometimes for assault. These people usually didn't fight the police but would protest as much as they dared to keep from being taken away. When people would see us arrest someone for being out of line it would usually make them realize it wasn't worth going to jail for and they would calm down. An uprising would flare up somewhere else in the stadium.

Escorting someone up the stairs to an exit while they were trying to pull away and explain it wasn't their fault, someone was picking on the, that I turned my ankle on the steps. It really didn't hurt much at the time in fact I finished out my duties through my watch. Afterward, doing paperwork at the station house, my ankle began to throb and swell. By the time I got home, I had to cut my boot off.

After a sleepless night, I went to the doctor first thing the next morning. He x-rayed and found bone-chip in my ankle joint. Before I knew it I was in surgery that put me off work for some time. Just as I was thinking I could go back to work, there was another surgery.

Then came light duty. Now I was assigned to Metro desk and worked the radio. Metro and SWAT had their own radio and was dispatched from our office. For sometimes because of the nature of our missions, we wouldn't want everyone in the city to know where or what assignments we were working on. I now worked morning watch, sometimes by myself. I was the watch commander, the radio operator and took care of any problems that came in.

This job was very important, because when there was a SWAT call I would direct my team and keep everyone informed of what was going on. It would be my decision to determine if there was a SWAT call up at all. This job is one I really felt uncomfortable with and in fact I downright hated it. I was a street cop. I would tell everyone who would listen, "I want to be out where the action is. Not behind this radio and desk."

Every month I continued to see my doctor, thinking I would be put back on full duty but this wasn't going to happen. There would be no more jumping; running or walking the streets I'd grown to miss. For the first time in my career I was really unhappy. I heard all the street stories and received the details secondhand. Now I wasn't part of the job I loved.

While talking to some other officers and supervisors, telling them my feelings, I was advised to put in for my pension. I did and it was granted. It was not a happy day for I knew I would never wear blue again. It was truly my honor to serve on the best police department in the world. During my career, 33 police officers gave their lives in the line of duty—no higher sacrifice can be made. I am truly proud to have once been a part of that thin blue line that stands between good and evil and right and wrong.

There are people in this great land of ours that are always willing to throw stones and point fingers, and Monday morning quarterback LAPD in particular, as well as other police departments and officers for doing a thankless job. I worked with these fine men and women. I'm sure when you have so many there are going to be a few bad apples but I never saw, heard or witnessed anything but the brave, honest and proud officers who stood daily in the line of fire, for their employer, the people of Los Angeles.

After the Rodney King riots, the city fathers let Darryl Gates retire. He was one of the best chiefs of police in the history of the Los Angeles police department. Up until this time every chief came up through the ranks, so they knew what it was like walking a beat, working vice, working patrol, they had been there and done that. They never asked anything of any of the officers they hadn't done themselves.

But now the city fathers saw fit to go outside the city and hire a chief unfit to lead fine police officers and had no knowledge of the city whatsoever. The city fathers went to Philadelphia where they found Willy Williams, a man with a high school education. Williams could not even pass the peace officers' standard training requirements for the state of California and was denied peace officers status under the law. He wasn't even legally allowed to carry a firearm.

Due to this action, seasoned and experienced officers left the city in droves, through retirement and lateral transfers to other departments, because anyone would take an LAPD officer, knowing their training was the best in the world.

With an immediate need for officers to fill the void, a drop in standards occurred which resulted in hiring individuals without the mental evaluations or the background checks, causing officers who were not capable of being prepared for the duties they would incur, including Rafael Perez and David Mack and others of their ilk. Perez once tried to become an officer in the city of Chino, California, turned down by that department as being unfit. Perez ended up blacking the eye of the LAPD with his drug stealing and corruption. Mack became a bank robber. Both, like Williams, made Las Vegas their playground.

I feel due to this poor judgment on the part of management the fine citizens of Los Angeles are now paying the piper. All the great policemen in the city of Los Angeles have been shamed. Now good sense has prevailed and once again they have a chief that came up through the ranks and I'm hoping his knowledge and good judgment will prevail, once again restoring the honor and number one rating of the best police department in the world, the LAPD.

I want to thank the people of Los Angeles and South Los Angeles in particular, for that is where I spent most of my time, for letting me work for you and come into your homes and neighborhoods while serving and protecting you.

For this I remain Forever Blue.

Epilogue

A Chance Meeting

Janet Warford-Perry

I met Bill Myers in 1992 while covering the hard news beat for a small daily newspaper in northeast Oklahoma. Bill worked lake patrol for the Grand River Dam Authority and I would contact him for comment about boating accidents he worked on Grand Lake O' the Cherokees.

During one conversation, I casually mentioned that Bill seemed more at ease talking to the press than most police officers did. "Oh, I learned to love the press when I worked for the Los Angeles Police Department," Bill said casually relaying his encounters in the media limelight.

A few months later, when National Police Week rolled around, Bill agreed to let me write a feature story about his career, in particular, his involvement with Patty Hearst and the SLA shooting. Many readers responded favorably to that article, most indicating they had no idea about Bill's colorful background.

After the article appeared in print, Bill confided to me that he'd always wanted to write a book about his career experiences but felt he didn't have the writing skills to put the words onto paper. He said he felt like I was the person that could turn the stories into published form. To say that Bill had more faith in my talent than I did is an understatement.

An avid reader of true-crime novels, I was certain of one thing. The material Bill had to present was the type of subject matter that made for good reading. Thus, in 1993 I agreed to co-author the novel, figuring at that time it was only a gesture he had made to compliment a struggling writer.

But I underestimated Bill's genuine sincerity and dedication to get the story out of his head and put into words. He did not forget that conversation and the during the next few years would often remind, "we need to start writing our book."

During the years of 1995-98 I had been promoted to news editor and demands of my occupation left little time for regular sleep, much less writing a book on the side.

But in the spring of 1998, I had been assigned a job as general manager of a weekly newspaper in Jay, Oklahoma, and a much less demanding position within the company.

Bill appeared at my office one day and announced, "We're going to write that book. I've got a name picked out, we're going to call it *Forever Blue*."

Plans were made that once a week, Bill would meet at my office for lunch and dictate the stories while I typed them into a laptop computer. Every Wednesday at noon, also a slow day at the paper, we could be found working on the book.

Several times other employees would stop to listen as the stories unfolded. I wondered if this would provide too much of a distraction. However, when piecing the notes together, it seemed the more of an audience that gathered the more colorful and real Bill's adventurous accounts became.

The foundation for the book was completed during the summer of 1998, just weeks before I lost my 17-year-old son to suicide. It seemed for a time, I would be the one to remain forever blue.

But writing the book had helped to form a bond between an unlikely pair. It was as if the training Bill received at the LAPD automatically kicked in as he took me under his wing and patiently waited the storm out. Each week at the regularly scheduled meeting time, Bill would bring me lunch, or take me to a local restaurant, offering kind words of condolence suggesting ways to "get back off that horse that threw you."

During the fall of 1999, a twist of fate provided the boost needed to spur on the writing of Forever Blue. Owners of the financially struggling newspaper decided to close the doors and cease publication. I chose to enter freelance writing, thus allowing much more time to concentrate on a novel.

Knowing Bill hated the holiday season because of the violence he'd witnessed during his career, during Christmas of 1999, I made a promise to finish the book as a holiday gift to my friend. It was the least I could do for a man who patiently waited for over a year while nary a word was written.

It should also be noted that both our spouses became staunch supporters of the book in a very passive manner during this time period. Neither Lupe, nor my husband Keith, ever complained that too much time was being spent on the book, and graciously accepted the barrage of phone calls back and forth or the e-mails that furiously flew from one house to another. It seemed as though our spouses had become silent partners, occasionally asking how it was going, but never fussing over the long hours required to complete the task.

As people across the world rang in the new millennium, Bill and I polished Forever Blue and the book was ready for the press in March of 2000. Whether or not the book ever sells one copy, the friendship that evolved between two families during the writing process is sure to continue for a lifetime.

—Janet Warford-Perry

Order additional autographed first edition copies of *Forever Blue* today by completing the following information:

Name: _____

Address: _____

City: _____

State: _____ *Zip Code:* _____

Please allow 4-6 weeks for delivery

Mail form along with your check or money order for $25.95 (US currency) to:
Forever Blue
P.O. Box 588
Afton, OK 74331

Oklahoma residents must include an additional 4.5% sales tax